RE/ARCHITECTURE

Old Buildings / New Uses

RE/ARCHITECTURE

Old Buildings / New Uses

With 306 illustrations, 50 in color

Sherban Cantacuzino

Abbeville Press · Publishers · New York

On the title page: *Dining room in the Charles Street Meeting House, Boston: a Baptist church that has been imaginatively transformed into an architect's home, offices and shops.*

Photographic credits   The following abbreviations have been used: *a*, above; *b*, below; *r*, right; *l*, left. Abbey of Saint-Wandrille 194; Aga Khan Award for Architecture 72–3; *Architects' Journal* 146–51; Architectural Press 58*b*, 90*a*; Arthur Cotton Moore Assoc. 17; Arup Assoc. 206–9; BASA Architects 204–5; Benjamin Thompson Assoc. 120*a*; Dave Bower 80–1; Crispin Boyle 207; George M. Bramall 182–3; Brunning Advertising and Marketing (West) Ltd 88*a*; Richard Bryant 103, 104*r*, 105, 146–51, 159, 161; Bundesdenkmalamt 92–3; J. D. Burton 97; Business Design Centre 90*b*; S. Cantacuzino 35*l*, 36–7, 56, 57*a*, 60, 99*al*, 189*r*, 191, 195; Mario Carrieri 54, 68*r*, 69–71; Lluís Casals 200, 203; Martin Charles 16*a*, 90*a*, 104*l*, 106*al*; Charles Robertson Partnership 162–3; City of Constance 188, 189*l*; Cesare Colombo 64–7, 165–7; Peter Cook 148–51; COOPARCH s.c.r.l. 96; Mark C. Darley 157*al*; Christophe Demonfaucon 112; Farrokh Derakhshani 72–3; John Donat 58*a*, 82–5; Ford, Powell and Carson 173; Bengt Forser 89*b*; Robert Galbraith 57*b*; Rick Gardner· Houston 14, 114; Jonathan M. Gibson 216*b*; La Goélette 194; Graham Gund Assoc. 46*a*; Lars Hallén 86, 108–11; Hallmark Photographs 198–9; Harlan Hambright and Assoc. 16*b*; Hickey-Robertson 115–17; James Higgins 132–5; Alastair Hunter 126, 136–9; Timothy Hursley 160; IDP Interiors Disseny 192, 200–3; Konrad Keller 190*l*; Keyes, Condon and Florance 130*b*; The Lace Hall, Nottingham 172*a*; Ola Laiho 40–5; Renzo Lupi 64–7; Arthur Martin 178–9; William E. Mathis 10*b*, 26–9; Peter McCormack 15; John Mills 106*bl* and *r*, 107; The Viscount Moore 215, 216*a*, 217; National Monuments Record 58*b*; Niall Phillips Assoc. 129; Olympia and York 8; Frank Pedrick 124–5; Gérard Pétremand 98, 99*r*–101; Phillips and Ryburn 131; David Pickman 156, 157*ar*; Stephen P. Rayment 38–9; Mocho Riego 30–3; Siho Rista 130*a*; P. Robino 61–3; Steve Rosenthal 2–3, 46*bl* and *r*, 47, 52–3, 118–19, 120*b*, 121–3, 174–7; Aarno Ruusuvuori 10*a*, 18–21; St George's Music Trust 171; Philip Sayer 180–1; Deidi von Schaewen 12, 22–5, 89*a*, 113; Scottish Development Department 210–13; Roland Simounet 76–9; Richard Squires 196–7; Georg Stärk 9, 141–5; Jessica Strang 94–5; Dahliette Sucheyre 91; Hüsrev Tayla 74–5; Terry Farrell Partnership 88*b*; J. W. Thomas 172*b*; Rosi Troxler 48–51; Nick Wheeler 34, 35*r*, 152–5.

Please note that throughout the text "first floor" refers to the floor above ground floor, in accordance with British usage.

Library of Congress Cataloging-in-Publication Data

Cantacuzino, Sherban.
     Re-architecture: old buildings/new uses/Sherban Cantacuzino.
         p.   cm.
     Bibliography: p.
     Includes index.
     ISBN 1–55859–006–4
     1. Buildings–Remodeling for other use.   I. Title.
NA2793.C35   1989
720′.28′6–dc20
                                                                    89–6688
                                                                      CIP

First American edition

Contents

Commercial Buildings

Types 88

Bank · Depot · Market hall · Abattoir · Warehouse · Seaport · Lighthouse

Schemes

Industrial Buildings

Types 128

Mill · Brewery · Industrial plant · Factory

Schemes

5 Ecclesiastical Buildings

Types   170

Meeting house · Temple · Church · Priory · Monastery

Schemes

6 Rural Buildings

Types   194

Farmhouse · Barn · Granary · Hunting lodge · Menagerie

Schemes

Introduction
The Tradition of Changing Use

There is nothing new about buildings changing their function. Because structure tends to outlive function, buildings throughout history have been adapted to all sorts of new uses. Except when the cataclysm of natural forces or war wreaked wholesale destruction, change in the urban fabric was slow, which enabled generation after generation to derive a sense of continuity and stability from its physical surroundings. Even when buildings were abandoned, pilfered for materials or condemned for political reasons, the process of attrition was slow and incomplete compared with modern methods of demolition. The Roman arena at Nîmes in the South of France became a small fortified town in the early Middle Ages, while Diocletian's vast palace at Spalato (Split) in Croatia became a cathedral and housing for the inhabitants of the town, and has remained so to this day. In fact, until the Industrial Revolution the common pattern was for buildings to be adapted to new uses; only since then has it become more usual to demolish and build new.

After the Second World War the pace of change accelerated to such an extent that redundancy, followed by demolition, became commonplace in urban areas. Planning policies caused the departure of industrial and commercial activities from central areas to the suburban or rural zones that had been allocated exclusively to them. Buildings that had housed these activities, such as warehouses and malthouses, now stood on increasingly valuable land, so many were demolished to make way for more profitable development, such as shopping centres and offices. In Britain and in Europe the post-War years also witnessed the construction of a great deal of public housing, built by local authorities in the form of housing estates, which encircled the towns like a mushroom growth and caused the dereliction of the existing central urban housing stock. As people moved to the new suburbs, they left churches and other community buildings in the centre without a role and doomed to redundancy, dereliction and often demolition. In Britain and the United States the Garden City movement at the turn of the century had already idealized suburbia and created a taste for suburban living, so a process that was started by private initiative and later encouraged by public authorities continued unabated in the hands of housing developers.

In the last twenty years there has been a gradual and welcome reversal of this trend. In Britain the Civic Amenities Act of 1967 broke new ground by requiring local authorities to designate conservation areas, and encouraged other countries to introduce similar legislation. If the Act recognized that there was more to conservation than looking after individual buildings of architectural and historical importance, it took a few more years before public opinion, incensed by the repeated loss of familiar landmarks and by the low quality of so much of the new architecture, grasped the importance of group value and area conservation. Today it is generally accepted in Western Europe and America that conservation policy, of which finding new uses for old buildings is a part, must be integral with planning policy. Having a planning policy at all, however, is unpopular in the more empirically minded Anglo-Saxon countries because the planning of the 1950s and 1960s is considered to have failed. Conservative governments seem to prefer to be guided by market forces, even to the degree of making the developer responsible for providing the infrastructure of roads and services.

The lack of planning as it affects conservation is well illustrated by London's Canary Wharf development on the Isle of Dogs. The planning authority, the London Docklands Development Corporation, should have safeguarded the historic Greenwich Hospital axis on the one hand, and protected the eighteenth-century West India Dock warehouse on the other. Instead, it reacted favourably to a massive development which included three skyscrapers set originally on the Greenwich axis and overwhelming the Grade 1 listed warehouse on the other side of the dock. Even the usually logical French failed to foresee the disastrous effect of the skyscraper development at La Défense on the impressive vista up the Champs-Elysées to the Arc de Triomphe. True conservation means not only converting old buildings to appropriate new uses, but also protecting their setting.

It is axiomatic that to be able to pursue an active conservation policy, a planning authority must have full knowledge of what it is conserving. Perhaps in collaboration with local amenity societies, art colleges or architectural schools, it must examine and classify the building stock in each area; identify the danger points and anticipate redundancy; prepare strict criteria for sympathetic redevelopment if the building is dispensable; or, alternatively, propose appropriate new uses or other means of preservation; and document buildings by measuring, analysing and photographing them.

The emphasis in converting buildings to new uses has shifted most recently from the historic building and the problem of extending its life, to the challenge of using existing space in more ordinary, though often listed buildings which are solidly built and adaptable, and which are often of industrial or commercial origin. The emphasis has also shifted from accurate and reverential restoration to a freer and more creative attitude to the changes that an old building may undergo; from the building as art object to the building as the product of a whole socio-economic system.

In practice, this has meant that we no longer concentrate only on the architectural and historic merit of threatened buildings but see the whole stock of existing buildings as potentially useful for sound economic, social and ecological reasons, and as an opportunity for urban regeneration. It has meant that we no longer focus only on the restoration of an individual monument, but attend to the conservation of whole areas. It has meant that we now look beyond the individual church or country house, at warehouses, mills, factories, market halls and other industrial and commercial buildings. It has meant, too, that instead of looking for public uses like museums and art galleries, we now also look for commercial uses; and we can now convert large buildings, which are unlikely ever to attract single users again, into workspace for small firms, into several housing units, or into a mix of uses.

This book includes a great many examples of buildings that have been converted to commercial purposes. It also includes a number of examples that are part of a larger urban regeneration programme. The conversion of a large warehouse in Galveston, Texas, into a hotel is part of a concerted effort to revive the fortunes of the nineteenth-century commercial centre. In Lowell, Massachusetts, the Lowell Mill was the first of several very grand mills to be converted as part of a plan to revive the whole city, while the rehabilitation of the Albert Dock in Liverpool is part of the Merseyside Development Corporation's plans for the whole dock area. There are also several examples of very large buildings or groups of buildings that have been converted to mixed uses, such as the Petershausen Monastery in Constance or the Tiefenbrunnen flour mill in Zurich.

As the conversions described here were drawn from so many different countries and were carried out over a decade, it has proved impossible to give the cost of the work in any meaningful way. Ten years ago there was evidence that the cost of converting old buildings consistently outstripped the cost of

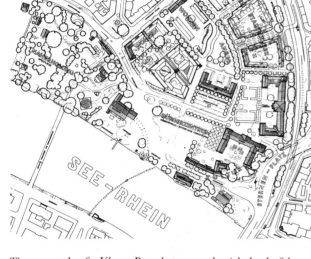

The master plan for Kloster Petershausen on the right bank of the Rhine at Constance. The priory buildings and later barracks are being converted to new uses, and new buildings are being added to create an administrative, social and cultural centre in a run-down part of the city.

The Tiefenbrunnen mill at Zollikon, a lake-side suburb of Zurich. Its nucleus consists of two parallel buildings with a pedestrian street between. The redundant flour mill has been converted to mixed uses, including housing, shops, offices, and light industry.

In renovating the City Hall block in Helsinki, the eighteenth- and early nineteenth-century perimeter buildings facing the streets have been preserved and converted into shops at ground level and offices above. Inside the block, on the other hand, accretions have been removed to provide space for new buildings and to reveal the important old buildings.

The vast and magnificent Union Station in St Louis functioned as a railway station from 1894 until 1978. In 1976 it was designated a National Historic Landmark and has since been converted into a shopping centre and hotel.

equivalent new work. This tendency appears to have been reversed, and conversions are now fully competitive. In addition, more developers have learnt to appreciate the unquantifiable values of age, character and architectural quality, and have discovered that people will pay more to be in an old building, where space standards, not to mention architectural quality, are much higher than they would be in an equivalent new building. It is perfectly possible, moreover, to carry out a conversion by phasing, as has been done in the case of the City Hall block in Helsinki, or by cutting back on some aspects of the work to allow unexpected costs to be covered. 'You never really know', a recent British government-sponsored publication points out, 'what you are going to find next with an old building, but if you really keep your eyes open, you can see ways of saving money just as much as spending it.'

What has also helped is the fact that over the years more government money has been made available for conservation, in the form of loans and grants, at both national and local level. Nevertheless, there is still much that governments could do to provide financial incentives. For instance, in Britain repair and maintenance work to all buildings, including listed buildings, is at present charged Value Added Tax (VAT) at the standard rate of 15 per cent, while major works of alteration or reconstruction to listed buildings are zero-rated. There is therefore a positive incentive substantially to alter, renew and, inevitably, damage listed buildings. This is one reason why listed buildings are often totally reconstructed within the existing outer shell, making a travesty of conservation.

No exemption is applied to listed buildings by any of the EEC member states – indeed, many of them charge well above 15 per cent. Belgium, Spain, Italy and Portugal have two rates, the lower rate applying to residential buildings, historic buildings or public works, but of all the countries in Europe it is probably the Netherlands that provide something like a model, though Belgium, Germany and the Scandinavian countries have similar tax incentive schemes. There is a yearly fund, part of a seven-year rolling programme, which is four times the amount *per capita* spent on conservation in Britain. It is administered jointly by central and local government, and includes the maintenance and repair of all major monuments, mills and historic properties, as well as urban renovation schemes. Major incentives are tax-deductible interest on repair and upkeep costs of historic buildings.

Like the Dutch system, the American system also combines the benefit of grants with that of tax relief. The 1966 Historic Preservation Act voted a yearly sum to provide grants to owners of registered properties and encouraged the re-use of old buildings in a number of ways. The 1976 Tax Reform Act introduced tax concessions on the costs of renovation and reduced existing tax incentives to replace old buildings with new. As a result of the 1981 Economic Recovery Tax Act, private investors were able to obtain a tax credit of up to 25 per cent on the capital cost of converting an old building, providing it was of landmark status. The result was a great upsurge in the adaptation of old buildings to new uses and explains why nearly one-quarter of the book consists of American examples. Without these incentives it would have been impossible, for instance, to restore and convert the enormous Union Station in St Louis. Unfortunately, there was also abuse of the tax credit system, which the 1986 Tax Reform Act has endeavoured to correct, with the result that in 1987 the number of rehabilitation projects declined by 35 per cent. America has also led the way in showing how conservation can be financed by a combination of different sources, with public finance being used to attract private investment, for example. Britain's Urban Development Grant is based on this principle and its success indicates that joint ventures of public and private funds are being accepted as a satisfactory *modus operandi*.

The economic argument for rehabilitation or conversion is a powerful one, for most of the examples illustrated are not just concerned with maintaining the fabric of an old building, but introduce completely new environmental standards and services. Conversion work is labour-intensive, employing thousands of small builders, whereas new building tends to be capital-intensive. New building is energy-consuming, where conversion work is energy-saving. And old buildings are themselves energy-saving because of their massive construction and small windows.

So there is everything to be said for extending the life of old buildings by converting them to new uses. Writing in 1971, Dr P.A. Stone pointed out that 'urban quality depends more on the standard of maintenance and improvement of existing stock than on the standards to which new stock is built', because the annual addition to the stock is proportionally very small. The division of national resources between new building and maintenance ought, he argued, to be nearer 50:50 than the 75:25 that it was in Britain at the time of writing. It is gratifying to record that eighteen years later, this division of national resources is indeed nearer the proportion that it ought to be. Even with the present increase in new building, it is likely to become even more so.

The six chapters into which the book is divided represent six different categories of building, each of which contains several distinct building types. Under *Private Buildings*, for instance, there is the castle, the palace, the town house and the country house. The emphasis is therefore on the building type before conversion. The original character of the building is stressed, together with the challenge to the developer and architect to preserve as much of this character as possible in the conversion. The examples illustrated were selected for three main reasons: for their visual importance in the urban or rural context; for the social or cultural importance of their new use; and for the design quality of the conversion.

The fifty-four examples studied in detail are taken from fifteen countries. The USA and the UK are especially prominent, but this simply reflects the great wealth of nineteenth-century industrial buildings that exist on both sides of the Atlantic. Nearly half the book is thus devoted to conversion of buildings belonging to what has been named the *functional tradition*, within which – as J.M. Richards has put it – 'new and more sophisticated standards are achieved gradually and unselfconsciously as one anonymous mind after another applies itself to the improvement or modification of an established pattern'. Finding new uses for these buildings is important not only because of their intrinsic worth, but also because the very act of converting them may teach today's architects something about this established pattern. The conversion of a textile mill or a warehouse, moreover, offers considerably more freedom than the conversion of a medieval church or an eighteenth-century country house, buildings of outstanding architectural importance that require scholarly restoration and inhibit the choice of a new use.

Evidence of a swing to conservation comes from the architects themselves. Even ten years ago few of the best-established architects were prepared to devote their talents to conversion work. Now it is otherwise, as the galaxy of names – Rogers, Stirling, Martorell, Bohigas and Mackay among them – testifies.

1

Public Buildings

City hall

Railway station

Hospital

Corn exchange

Observatory

Courthouse

School

The great vault of the Gare d'Orsay in Paris now houses a national museum illustrating the flowering of the arts that took place between 1850 and 1914 – including what has come to be called 'the other nineteenth century', the 'lost' tradition of Salon art, to which the winged figure of the Archangel Michael belongs. The magnificent clock over the entrance to the museum is the original station clock, which has been fully restored.

Public buildings are those built either by the government or by private enterprise for the benefit of the public, and are normally accessible to the public. There are many categories of public building, and this chapter does not profess to be exhaustive. Rather than take each building type in turn – town hall, railway station, hospital, school, etc. – it is best to group together several building types with common characteristics.

Perhaps the largest category is the building with one or more grand spaces, the form of which is determined by their function. It is important that in converting such buildings to new uses, these spaces are not subdivided, and that the structure, if visible, is not covered up or its integrity compromised in any way. In this category come courthouses, observatories, stock exchanges, corn and cotton exchanges, and railway stations. Included in this chapter are the courthouses in east Cambridge, USA (p. 46), one of which has had its courtrooms converted into open-plan offices, while another now houses the studios, galleries and theatre of an arts centre. The functional requirements of a theatre are not ideal for a finely decorated room, but such visually intrusive elements as the stage platform or lighting equipment can always be removed and the room returned to its pristine state.

Observatories and exchanges consist essentially of one grand space, and ancillary accommodation in cellular form. It is this ancillary accommodation that is usually found to be inadequate when searching for a new use, though solutions to the problem can often be found. At the Vartiovuori Observatory in Turku (p.40) there was fortunately a separate building, an old water tank, that could provide storage and exhibition space for the museum into which the observatory has been converted. At Cambridge, UK, additional accommodation had to be built on the very restricted site of the old Corn Exchange to provide the back-up facilities necessary for a multi-purpose hall (p. 38).

Railway stations usually consist of two separate structures: the shed and the head house. The shed is one vast space in which the structure and, often, its subdivision into clearly defined bays play an important part. The head house is mainly cellular but also incorporates the booking hall and other grand spaces, usually associated with a hotel. It is clear from the two examples illustrated in this chapter, the Gare d'Orsay in Paris (p. 22) and the Union Station in St Louis (p. 26), that a hotel and shopping centre are better suited than a museum, which needs a variety of spaces, from the very intimate to the very grand, rather than one vast and imposing space. To make the shed of the Gare d'Orsay suitable for a museum, a substantial structure of platforms and smaller spaces had to be inserted. The objection is not so much to the principle of this additional structure, but to its design and ponderous character, which diminish the simple grandeur of the shed.

The St Louis station no longer serves the railway, Amtrak, which could have continued to use a small part of it, but preferred to go elsewhere instead. Many railway stations in America have been converted to new uses, but many of these also continue to function as a railway station in a reduced way. The Union Station at Indianapolis, a magnificent neo-Romanesque structure that preceded the St Louis station by a few years, has been converted into a commercial complex, but also remains a mass-transit station. The same is true of the Union Station in Dallas, a more modest 1930s building in the Art Deco style, which has been converted into restaurants, bars, cafés, small shops and rooms for hire. Another station that has retained its original function is the Santa Fe railway station in Galveston, an eleven-storey office building incorporating the station booking hall, built in 1913 and extended in

The Santa Fe railway station in Galveston, Texas, has been converted into the Shearn Moody Plaza, a museum of transportation and commerce with offices above by Ford, Powell and Carson.

1931 as the headquarters of the Sante Fe Railroad Company. The booking hall and some of the open platforms and tracks behind have been converted into a museum of transportation and commerce, while the rest of the building now provides offices for public agencies, and facilities for the University of Texas Medical Branch and for Galveston Community College. The head house of Dearborn Station in Chicago, built in 1883 to the designs of the New York architect Cyrus Eidlitz, has been converted into offices and forms the entrance to a two-level shopping mall that has been erected over the tracks at the back.

In England a number of small country stations are now private houses and several have been converted into museums and visitors' centres. One of the more spectacular examples is the 1838 Curzon Street Station in Birmingham, a grand head house with a giant portico of Ionic columns and a large central booking hall which rises the full height of the building. Curzon Street Station was built as the northern terminus of Stephenson's London and Birmingham Railway, but became a goods depot in 1852 when a new passenger station was opened at New Street. In 1979, when the building was in a semi-derelict condition, British Rail donated it to Birmingham Council, which immediately set about restoring and converting it into training workshops and voluntary organization offices. Curzon Street Station lost its shed a long time ago. Central Station, Manchester, by contrast, is all train shed and no head house, because the hotel that was to have been built in front of the shed never materialized, so that, unlike St Pancras Station in London, the full span of the great arched roof can still be seen from the road. Greater Manchester Council and Commercial Union, with help from central government, have converted the shed into an exhibition centre as part of the city council's programme of action in industrial and commercial areas. It aims to improve the environment and to raise the level of economic activity, and so increase job opportunities in selected parts of the city.

A second category of public building includes structures that are essentially cellular, but contain ceremonial rooms, the integrity of which must be respected in any conversion. The city or town hall is a building type that falls into this category, a fine example being the City Hall in Helsinki (p. 18), whose ceremonial rooms have been beautifully restored. In London, following the abolition of the Greater London Council, there have been several proposals for the conversion of County Hall, an imposing, classically inspired riverside building, designed by Ralph Knott in 1911 but only completed in 1933. Finding suitable new uses for its fine ceremonial rooms remains a matter of concern.

A third category is the building that is predominantly cellular, often with many spacious rooms. Into this category fall schools, hospitals and barracks – all essentially functional buildings for which it is generally not difficult to find new uses. An example that is neither quite a school, nor quite a hospital is the Hospice of San Michele in Rome (p.36), which was both an institution for orphans, the poor and the aged, and also a prison. A vast building strung out along the Tiber, it has been converted mostly to office use, but includes an imaginatively conceived conference centre in the roof space above the church.

Population movement, demographic change and rationalization have caused the redundancy of many school buildings all over the world. In England small country schools have been converted successfully into private houses. The Charles Sumner School in Washington, a public school for black children, built in 1872 to the designs of Adolph Cluss, became redundant

Central Station in Manchester (UK), converted into an exhibition centre by Jack Bogle of EGS Design.

The new canteen in the county constabulary headquarters at Netley in Hampshire, a conversion from a Victorian mental hospital by the county architect, Colin Stansfield-Smith.

The Pension Building in Washington D.C. converted into the National Building Museum and government offices by Keyes, Condon and Florance, with Giorgio Cavaglieri as associate architect.

when the school moved elsewhere in 1979. Used for a while as offices, then threatened with demolition, this fine building was finally saved and converted into a museum of black education and a community centre for blacks, which contains meeting and exhibition rooms, and an auditorium. The developer who undertook the work was allowed to build on some of the school's land in return for helping to finance the Sumner School Museum and Archives – a prime example of how compromises can be made between commercial and cultural interests. In Baltimore there are two large schools which have been converted to new uses. The former Loyola College and High School, part of a Jesuit foundation that includes the church of St Ignatius and was built variously between 1840 and 1899. It was taken over in 1975 by Baltimore's resident professional theatre, Center Stage, and converted into a 500-seat theatre, with a partial thrust-stage, foyer, rehearsal room, scene and costume shop, green room and dressing rooms. A second phase will provide a 350-seat proscenium theatre, a restaurant, classrooms, workshop and studio area; and a final phase plans an outdoor courtyard theatre and simple apartments for guest artists.

Like schools, many hospitals are becoming redundant, because medical advances and changes in attitudes and practice have caused new hospitals to be built. In Madrid the Hospital de San Francisco de Paula de Jornaleros, an enormous pile planned around a central courtyard with four radiating wings, an entrance building and a church (completed in 1917 to the designs of Antonio Palacios), has been converted into public offices. In Sweden an asylum at Vadstena has been made into apartments, and in London two of the old central hospitals whose function has moved to suburban locations, St George's and Charing Cross, are now being converted, the first into a luxury hotel and the second into a police headquarters. Another hospital that has become the headquarters of the county constabulary is the old mental hospital, part of the now demolished Royal Victoria Military Hospital at Netley in Hampshire. A rather special case is the former Istituto di Riposo per la Vecchiaia in Turin, built between 1882 and 1887 to house old people. This monumental hospital, which is constructed of load-bearing piers and vaults throughout its four storeys, each storey being 23 feet (7m) high, has been converted into offices for the Piedmontese Consortium for Information Data. The conversion tries to emphasize the original structural concept of vaulted bays supported on piers even where partitions and mezzanine floors have subdivided the space.

A particular building type not featured in the schemes that follow, which thrived in the United States and which is nowadays very popular, is the atrium building. Several floors of cellular accommodation are grouped around a central hall that rises through the full height of the building and is top-lit by a glass lantern. The form is inspired by Roman models but greatly enlarged. In the years after the Civil War General Montgomery C. Meigs of the Union Army visited Europe before designing the Pension Building in Washington, which is supposed to be based on the Palazzo Farnese in Rome. The 400-feet (122m) by 200-feet (61m) building was completed in 1887 and was occupied until 1926 by the Pension Bureau, which dispensed pensions to wounded veterans and relations of those killed in action in all American military conflicts. Its great hall, divided into three compartments by eight giant Corinthian columns, and one-and-a-half floors of the perimeter accommodation, now house the National Building Museum while other parts will be occupied by government offices, as they had been before a major restoration

The Old Post Office in Washington D.C., converted into a shopping and restaurant complex on the lower levels and into offices on the upper levels, by Arthur Cotton Moore Associates, with Benjamin Thompson Associates responsible for the shops and restaurants.

programme was begun in 1984. The museum holds regular exhibitions and has a publications progamme to bring to the attention of the public what is being designed and built in America. It organizes tours, lectures, school programmes and classes on the built environment for adults and children, and is building up an archive of drawings , photographs, models and artifacts.

Another atrium building, also in Washington, that has been given a brilliant new life is the Old Post Office, a neo-Romanesque pile completed in 1899 to the designs of the then Supervising Architect of the Treasury, Willoughby J. Edbrooke. In 1971 a permit for its demolition was approved, but well-organized preservationist forces and the expense of demolishing such a large and solidly built structure led in 1978 to its restoration and conversion into two distinct new uses: the three lower levels and the central hall were turned into a shopping and restaurant complex, and the perimeter accommodation has become offices.

The Edwardian baroque Police Building in New York, completed in 1909 to the designs of Hoppin and Koen, is a more conventional structure, occupying a whole city block, with a grand pedimented central bay crowned by a soaring drum, cupola and lantern, and end pavilions capped with flat domes. The central bay incorporates a lobby and monumental staircase, but this never rose through more than three full floors, the dome having always been a separate space accommodating the gymnasium and radio room. The police moved to new headquarters in 1973, but the future of the old building was protected by its designation as a New York City Landmark (1978) and its listing in the National Register of Historic Places (1980). In 1984 the city chose a developer, Fourth Jeffersonian Associates, who had received national acclaim for the renovation of Louis Sullivan's Guaranty Building in Buffalo, to restore and convert the building into luxury cooperative apartments.

Finally, mention should be made of theatres, cinemas and concert halls. These highly specialized buildings are not easily adaptable except to a similar use. Thus, Karl Friedrich Schinkel's Schauspielhaus of 1819 in Berlin, a theatre and opera house where Weber's *Der Freischütz* was given its first performance, has just been successfully converted into a concert hall. In San Antonio a cinema has become a performing arts centre, and in New York and Memphis cinemas have been converted into theatres. The difficulty of finding new uses for theatres is highlighted by the case of a turn-of-the-century theatre in north Chicago. Its ornate terracotta façade has been preserved, but everything behind the façade has been demolished and replaced with a multi-level shopping centre.

There is no doubt that it is easier to find a new use for the type of public building that is mainly cellular than for the type that contains large ceremonial rooms or, indeed, consists essentially of one or more grand spaces. Even then, the solid construction and finite nature of the internal spaces often make these buildings more difficult to convert than a nineteenth-century mill or warehouse, with their open floors and endless repetition of structural bays. Yet it is important and worthwhile to find new uses for public buildings when they become redundant, not only because they are often landmarks in their area, historically important and architecturally valuable, but also because they are soundly built, with a structure and envelope which it would be wasteful to destroy. It usually makes good economic sense, therefore, to preserve and adapt the town hall, courthouse, public library or railway station, when its original function has ceased, if only because of the solid construction and generous space, neither of which would ever be repeated in a new building.

City Hall block, Helsinki

Administrative quarter into multiple use

The city administration of Helsinki, Finland, has been a pioneer of rehabilitation. It began renovating and converting its real estate in 1959, beginning with the eastern side of Katariinankatu, and next holding an architectural competition, in 1960, for the two blocks between Katariinankatu and Unioninkatu. The southern half of one of these, the City Hall block, was completed in 1970, and included the restoration of the Great Hall, the construction of a new foyer under it, and the provision of a city boardroom and a mayor's suite. The northern half, only completed in 1988, involved the restoration of the Empire Hall and the construction of a new council chamber.

One of the main objectives of the renovation was to remove inappropriate accretions inside the block so as to provide space for new buildings, like the council chamber, and to reveal the important old buildings, such as the Empire Hall. The perimeter buildings facing the streets were mainly preserved and converted into shops at ground level with offices above. They date from the eighteenth century and were originally family houses, being known to this day as the Hellenius House or the Burtz House, for example.

Above: *View of the eastern courtyard, with the back of the old courthouse at the far end and the new building, housing the administration, council chamber and staff restaurant, on the left. The old courthouse and the wing on the right now house the information department on the ground floor, and reception and meeting rooms for the council members on the first and second floors.*

Right: *A corner of the new building shows how the modern expression of concrete and glass is quite compatible with the older buildings on the opposite side of the courtyard.*

Opposite: *The staircase in the old courthouse which leads to the Empire Hall.*

View of the City Hall block from the north, with Helsinki harbour in the background. The buildings facing Aleksanterinkatu are, from left to right, the old courthouse, the Burtz House and the Hellenius House. From Katariinkatu a ramp leads to 60 car-parking spaces located under the old basements.

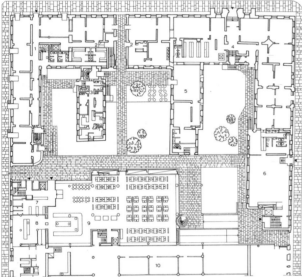

Above: *Ground-floor plan: 1 Hellenius House; 2 Burtz House; 3 Burtz House courtyard extension, 'Sumppu'; 4 old courthouse, formerly Bock House; 5 old courthouse courtyard extension with art gallery and Empire Hall on first floor; 6 city council information department; 7 Hellenius House side wing with entry to council chamber and staff restaurant; 8 kitchen; 9 new building with staff restaurant, and administration and council chamber above; 10 offices, which belong to the first phase of work completed in 1970.*

Opposite: *The Empire Hall restored. It was added 1816–19, when the Bock House was converted into a courthouse. It is now used by council members for receptions and other social functions.*

The northern half of the City Hall block consists essentially of three buildings. First, there is the corner building at 20 Aleksanterinkatu, formerly the Bock House. This was built in 1763 as a two-storey structure, but was converted into a courthouse by Carl Ludwig Engel between 1816 and 1819, when the third storey, Ionic portico and Empire Hall were added. Along Katariinankatu the façade dates from 1905, when this part of the building was virtually rebuilt. The new uses resulting from the recent conversion include storage in the vaulted cellars; entry for council members and an information section on the ground floor; and reception and meeting rooms for council members on the two floors above.

The second building is 22 Aleksanterinkatu, formerly the Burtz House. Dating from the third quarter of the eighteenth century, it was remodelled to the designs of Jean Wik in 1836, when the courtyard wing, known as Sumppu, was first built as a single-storey structure. Additional storeys were built in 1907, 1919 and 1952, and an attic floor was added to both the Burtz and the adjoining Hellenius House on the courtyard side in 1926. On the street side the building has been restored to its 1836 condition, with shops at ground-floor level and offices on the floors above. The ground floor and cellar of Sumppu have been converted into a restaurant, and the upper floors into offices. The whole wing was to have been demolished in the original 1960 scheme. The former Hellenius House at 24 Aleksanterinkatu was built in the 1760s as a two-storey structure, though Jean Wik added a third storey and restrained neo-classical decoration in 1835. The wing on Sofiankatu was partly remodelled during the first construction phase to provide an entrance, with the courtyard at street level and access to the council chamber and staff restaurant.

The scheme can be said to have two distinct parts: the buildings and courtyard wings on Aleksanterinkatu, which have been preserved and restored; and a section of new building in the middle of the block, which is linked to the first phase of construction. This core holds the administrative centre, the council chamber and the staff restaurant under it. Its architecture belongs emphatically to the present day and stands in contrast to the restored neo-classical buildings around it.

Gare d'Orsay, Paris

Station into national museum

The gently stepped central mall of the museum (right) is flanked by fortress-like walls which enclose smaller spaces and support galleries at first-floor level. The mall and galleries exhibit sculpture from Barye to Maillol; the spaces under the galleries contain paintings from Ingres and Delacroix to Manet and early Renoir. The twin towers at the end of the mall (below) contain exhibits of town planning and architecture, and in their bold form maintain the urban scale and character established by the mall. They also provide access to the Impressionist galleries, which have been inserted within the high roof on the river side, created by the architect of the station, Victor Laloux, to mask the vault of the station shed.

A large railway shed with a vaulted roof of single span, like the Gare d'Orsay in Paris, is not intrinsically suitable for a museum. So the first thing the architects of the conversion had to do was to find a way of providing as many smaller spaces as possible within the shed, while endeavouring to retain its integrity by not interfering with the vault. They did this by inserting below the springing of the vault a series of rooms and galleries spread over two levels, opening off a gently stepped central mall. At the lower level this mall is flanked by walls as strong as those of the quais along the Seine. It is all very positive – massive and chunky – and has been compared with a Cecil B. De Mille film set. The intention, according to the architects, was to establish a dialectic between the old and the new in which each is clearly recognizable. The architects have also remarked that, even if a railway shed is not best suited for a museum, a new building would never have permitted the creation of a sculpture gallery 115 feet (35m) high and 374 feet (114m) long.

The history of the Gare d'Orsay begins in 1897 when an architectural competition for a railway terminus on the corner of the Quai Anatole France and the rue de Bellechasse was won by Victor Laloux. The station was opened in 1900 and was one of the exhibits of the Exposition Universelle of that year. Its heyday came after the First World War when the number of people using the station doubled. But its platforms were too short and, despite the gradual electrification of the network, journeys to the provinces declined and

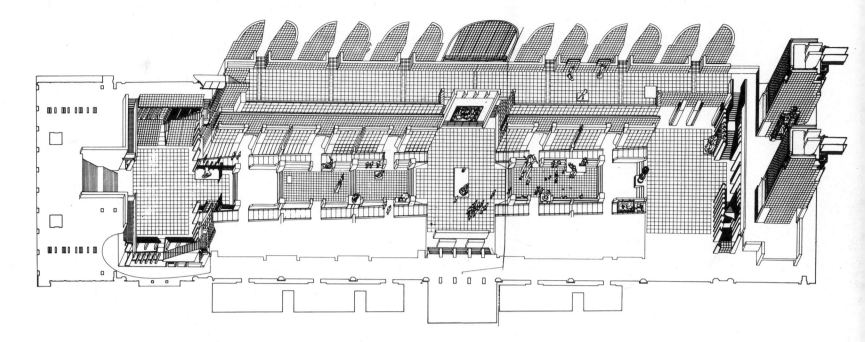

Top: *The exploded axonometric drawing shows, from left to right, the entrance to the museum from the rue de Bellechasse; the steps down to the central mall at the level of the former station platforms; the seven bays of the central mall with one of the flanking walls and upper galleries; and the twin towers at the end. It also shows how the flanking walls and upper galleries are interrupted at the fourth bay to form a cross-axis that did not exist in the original station.*

Above: *The west front, which now forms the entrance to the museum in the rue de Bellechasse. It was formerly the station hotel, and the entrance to the station was on the windy northern side facing the river. The large bronze in the forecourt is by Antoine-Louis Barye (1796–1875).*

suburban traffic increased. The station ceased operation altogether during the Second World War and never really picked up after the War, though it continued to serve suburban lines.

Among the many proposals made for the station after the War were its use as an air terminal, its demolition to make way for Air France offices and its conversion into a vast hotel. The last was the subject of an architectural competition that attracted many entries, some of which proposed the demolition of the old building. A movement to preserve the station was already under way, however, and in 1973 the building was listed and the hotel project abandoned. The Ministry of Cultural Affairs then bought the building from the French railway network, the SNCF, and presidential approval was given for its conversion into a museum of the nineteenth century. The competition for its conversion did not take place until 1979, and in the meantime some of the space was used first by Jean-Louis Barrault and his theatre company and later by the Drouot auction house.

In 1986 the old Gare d'Orsay was opened as the national museum for art and civilization covering the period 1850 to 1914. Entry is from the rue de Bellechasse, which is quieter and more protected than the long north side facing the Seine. Here the old hotel premises were also appropriate for accommodating the reception areas of the museum. To create a better relationship with the neighbourhood generally, the pavement on the south side (rue de Lille) has been raised and a public arcade formed. Also, on the south side two floors of former hotel bedrooms have been combined to form exhibition rooms opening on to the mall. On the river side, above the seven domes crowning the oval spaces of the former station concourse, a series of new galleries have been inserted for the Impressionist paintings previously in the Jeu de Paume. These galleries make use of empty roof space that originally had no other purpose than to hide the train shed from strollers in the Tuileries gardens across the river.

Above: *One of the first-floor galleries inserted within the series of domed oval bays on the river side, which were originally part of the station concourse. New stone screens partly fill the arches between the bays to provide hanging space for pictures.*

Right: *The former ballroom of the hotel has had its ornate plaster decoration restored and now contains white marble sculpture and paintings dating from the Third Republic.*

Union Station, St Louis, USA

Station into shopping centre and hotel

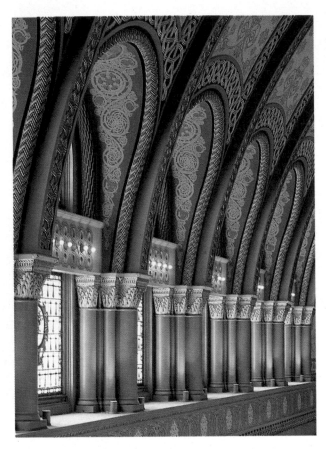

The Union Station's former main waiting room, now called the Grand Hall, serves as the lobby for the new hotel, but is also open to members of the public visiting the shopping centre. It was decorated by Louis Millet, who had worked for Louis Sullivan in Chicago before joining the architect of the station, Theodore C. Link, in St Louis. Within ten years of its completion it was painted over in solid colour, but it has now been meticulously restored to its original condition. Details like the capitals (right) bearing the arches over the windows (above) reveal the Romanesque and Byzantine influences that were current in the 1890s when the station was built.

The conversion in the early 1980s of the Union Station at St Louis, Missouri, into a shopping centre and a hotel (undertaken by Oppenheimer Properties, the Rouse Company and Omni International Hotels) is said to be the largest rehabilitation project of a historic building in America.

A competition for the design of the station in 1891, with architects chosen by invitation, was won by Theodore C. Link, and the station was opened three years later. It closed in 1978, but in its heyday (curiously enough, the 1940s – when the Gare d'Orsay closed altogether) 100,000 people a day passed through the terminal, which was serving 22 different railway lines. It is now once again a bustling place, even if the 150 retail outlets offer little more than novelty merchandise and recreational food.

The 750-feet-long (229m) and five-storeys-high station front, or headhouse, which is magnificently towered and turreted, originally contained a hotel, restaurants, shops, offices and, at its centre, the Grand Hall with its splendid barrel-vaulted ceiling. Many of these rooms continue to serve the same functions. The Grand Hall, for example, the station's sumptuously decorated former waiting room, now meticulously restored, has become the lobby for the new hotel, but remains open to the public as the formal entrance to the complex as a whole.

Immediately behind the headhouse is the concourse, which provides an ambulatory area, containing the minimum amount of retail (mainly in the form of kiosks), but with escalators, stairs and a bridge leading to the main shopping area and new hotel block under the train shed. Dimensions of 606 feet (185m) wide by 810 feet (247m) long by 140 feet (43m) high make this the largest train shed ever built. Because of its exceptional size, the area has been divided into 'neighborhoods', one of which is the new hotel block. Another 'neighborhood' is the two-level shopping area which runs at right-angles to the concourse at the east end of the shed. Restoration of the roof of the shed has been accompanied by reinforcement of its structure, but the wood, which used to cover it completely, making the former platform area rather dark, has been combined with clear glass, so that the space below is now vibrant with light.

The colour scheme of the Grand Hall (below and right) is predominantly green and gold, with touches of red and blue. The relief decoration over the arch in the end wall, which incorporates female figures holding torches, dramatizes the new use of electricity at the turn of the century.

The atrium of the old station hotel (bottom) has been restored and is now used as one of the circulation areas leading to the rooms of the new hotel, which are in the old building.

Above: *The magnificently towered and turreted headhouse, seen from the back, with part of the train shed on the right.*

Left: *The largest train shed in the world, covering 11½ acres, is divided into 'neighborhoods'. Here is the lake, with marketplace and beer garden on its shores. To the left is the car park, and to the right and behind (not visible) are the two-level shopping area and hotel. Light now pours in through the shed roof, the solid wood of the original cover having been replaced by clear glass.*

The Gothic Hall, evocative of the long galleries which are found in English country houses, has been restored and continues to form part of the hotel. It leads to an exquisite, small private dining room in the Adam style. The various styles found in the one building are evidence of the eclectic approach to design that was fashionable at the time.

Hospital de San Rafael, Santander, Spain

Hospital into seat of regional government

Above: *The open colonnade at ground-floor level which surrounds the central courtyard. The truncated pilasters indicate that the original building had a vaulted ceiling with arches between each bay. In the restoration a horizontal coffered ceiling has been substituted.*

The aerial view of the old hospital (above, right) *shows the roof lantern of steel and glass which transforms what was previously an open courtyard into a covered reception hall.*

The Hospital de San Rafael, built in 1791 to the designs of José Alday for Bishop Menéndez de Luarca, stands in the old centre of Santander, an area that long ago lost its vitality and became run down. The building itself ceased to be a hospital in 1928 and then housed a number of university faculties, falling increasingly into disrepair, until the loss of its roof made it all but a ruin and caused it to be abandoned. Although in 1962 there was a report on the restoration of the Hospital, there were no serious proposals until the building was eventually listed as a historic monument in 1980. It was then that the regional government of Cantabria decided to restore and convert it into the seat of the regional parliament, organizing a national architectural competition for the purpose in 1983.

Built of stone, the Hospital is a courtyard building where everything revolves around the central space. With the exception of the street front, which has an arcaded ground floor and simple classical ornament, the outer elevations are quite plain. On the courtyard side, on the other hand, there are continuous open colonnades and galleries on both floors. In converting the building, the courtyard was covered with a lightweight structure of steel and glass, spanning not between the colonnades, but between the walls running at the back of the open galleries. In this way an additional gallery has been created at attic level where the roof spaces have been brought into use as committee rooms, offices and a library, all vaulted and lit by new roof lights. The courtyard, meanwhile, has become a large reception hall.

The central entrance from the street suggested a semi-circular council chamber at the opposite end of the courtyard, with two new staircases on either side, connecting all the parts of the building, and especially linking the committee rooms on the top floor, the vestibules flanking the chamber and the cafeteria on the lower ground floor with the chamber itself. These staircases, as well as the chamber, are designed as separate structures which have no contact with the old walls of the hospital. The council chamber rises through three floors and sits over the cafeteria. From here there is access to the old water tank under the courtyard, which has been converted into a quiet retreat for the parliamentarians.

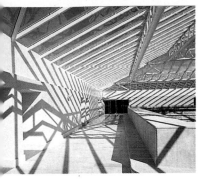

The courtyard in its derelict state before restoration (top), and after restoration and conversion with its new glass roof 'floating' over the top of the wall (right). The view of the newly formed second-floor gallery (above) shows how the glass roof takes its support from the wall at the back of the gallery, and why it therefore appears to float when seen from below.

Left: *A corner of the reception hall, or former courtyard. The central space and colonnades are sometimes used for art exhibitions. The large discs in the floor are glass covers to openings in the floor structure which let light into the basement areas.*

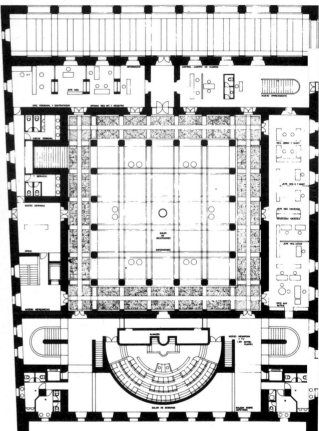

Above: *Ground-floor plan showing how the main entrance and council chamber, with its flanking staircases, impose a strong central axis that is not apparent from the four identical façades of the square reception hall. The plan also shows the arcaded portico on the street side which extends the full width of the building.*

The council chamber (above) has a stepped floor and is accessible from both ground-floor and first-floor level. Its volume is a half-cylinder, and the seating arrangement follows the curve concentrically. The walls and floor are lined with dressed stone. The council chamber sits on top of the cafeteria (right), which has a low ceiling that gains in height where the floor of the council chamber steps up.

Free Hospital for Women, Boston, USA

Hospital into luxury apartments

The main entrance block of the old hospital, which has been converted into luxury apartments – an eminently suitable use, since with its profusion of decorative features the building looks more like a country house than a hospital.

Brookline is a suburb of Boston, Massachusetts, and the Free Hospital for Women was built in one of its quiet residential areas, on the edge of Olmsted Park. This is part of the Emerald Necklace, a ten-mile-long chain of parks in Boston, designed by the great landscape architect Frederick Law Olmsted in the latter part of the nineteenth century. The original buildings were completed in 1895 to the designs of Shaw and Hunnewell, architects renowned locally for their elegant town houses and for their picturesque town hall at Wellesley. These buildings are made of pale orange-yellow brick, with limestone trim and a rusticated plinth of granite. The profusion of gables, arches and decorative features generally lend them the character of a country house rather than a hospital. As the establishment expanded, buildings were added by other architects which lacked the exuberance of the earlier buildings but which were nevertheless designed in sympathy with them.

The Free Hospital closed some years ago, and the buildings were left empty and neglected until Myerson/Allen and Company realized that the property was ideally situated for residential development. The Company then bought and converted it into 71 luxury apartments now called The Park. As was to be expected of a hospital, incongruous additions had been made in many places to the original buildings, and it was decided that any structures that added little to the character of the development should be demolished. Most of the buildings, however, were considered to be of historical significance, attractive, well built and with unusual interior spaces.

Five of the buildings, including the old boiler-house, have been converted into apartments varying from one- to three-bedroom, and from a mere 600 square feet (56m^2) to well over 2000 (186m^2). The interiors of these

On the south side the entrance block projects into the garden and terminates in a striking gable-ended façade, which has acquired an extra storey at the bottom because of the falling ground (above). Some of the apartments have double-height living rooms and bedrooms on an upper floor (right).

apartments preserve many of the original details: exposed wood trusses, fireplaces, mosaics and bas-relief plaster medallions. In addition, 16 new condominium apartments have been built beyond the old boiler-house to resemble a terrace of eight houses, each pair of houses sharing an entrance in a wide, projecting, gable-ended bay. In fact, the three storeys contain an apartment on the ground floor, raised on a terrace to allow car parking underneath, and a duplex on the two upper floors. The construction is in the same brick and slate roof covering used for the original hospital buildings. There is not a hint of modernity; instead, every effort has been made to fit into the surroundings. Mansard roofs and dormers, brick banding, changes of material and much decorative detail recall the style and scale of the neighbourhood as a whole, though inevitably, where the motor car rules the day, much of the landscape has had to be sacrificed to asphalted roads and parking lots.

Ospizio di San Michele, Rome

Hospice into offices and conference centre

The north side of the Cortile dei Ragazzi (children's court). The attic storey and the escape staircase are necessary, though unfortunate additions.

The Ospizio Apostolico di San Michele in the Ripa Grande in Rome is one of the largest buildings in a city of large buildings, and is prominently situated on the Tiber at the foot of the Aventine Hill. It is also of great historical and architectural importance, having had as its principal architects Carlo Fontana and Ferdinando Fuga, and having been the first building to combine, from the late seventeenth century onwards, the functions of a hospice for orphans and the aged with those of a prison and correction house.

Innocent XII, who founded San Michele, wanted to get the poor out of the habit of begging by putting them to work, so from the beginning wool- and linen-making, carpentry and book-binding were taught, followed by tapestry, printing and the establishment of a school of the liberal arts. With the decline of papal political authority in the middle of the nineteenth century, San Michele fell increasingly into disuse, and the teaching and manufacturing establishments were progressively closed. In 1938 the remaining staff were transferred to a new building, and only the two prisons at the southern end of the old hospice continued in use.

The Italian state acquired the building in 1969 with the intention of restoring it and converting it to new uses, but not before housing speculators had destroyed the neo-classical northern courtyard. The rest of the building was on the point of collapse, and the initial work consisted of consolidating the foundations and the structure where necessary, and making the building weatherproof by re-roofing. By 1981 the International Centre for Study of Preservation and Restoration of Cultural Property in Rome (ICCROM) had moved into the partly rebuilt northern courtyard and space had been created for exhibitions and conferences. In 1983 a section of the Ministry of Cultural and Environmental Property moved into the central part of the building, soon to be followed by the Central Institutes of Restoration and Documentation.

The unusually long building is planned around a series of courtyards, with the church at one end and the prisons at the other. Most of the work has been in the nature of a slow and painstaking restoration, with pleasing but unremarkable results. Over the barrel vaults of the cruciform church,

The old stenditoio *or clothes-drying area, which lies over the barrel vaults of the cruciform church, has been converted into a conference centre. Its cruciform area can be used as one or divided into two or three spaces by means of giant fans that fold away into the floor when not required* (right).

Above: One of the galleries surrounding the Cortile dei Vecchi (old people's court). This part of the building now provides offices for a government department.

however, the old *stenditoio* or clothes-drying area (literally, 'spreading out the clothes') has been converted into a spectacular conference centre. It consists of a cruciform area – a nave and two transepts – which can be used as one or divided into two or three rooms by means of semi-circular partitions in the form of enormous 'fans'; these fold away into the floor when not required. Between these fans and the arched structure holding up the roof there is fixed plate glass, which gives the space transparency even when the fans are in the 'up' position and the space is divided. The underside of the roof tiles and the timber roof trusses, strengthened in the restoration, are exposed throughout and provide a means of fixing the light-fittings. In the centre at the head of the 'nave', the seating and lectern are set on a rotating floor, and at the foot of the 'nave' there are booths for projection and simultaneous translation, which are kept clear of the roof structure in order to respect its integrity.

Corn Exchange, Cambridge, UK

Corn exchange into multi-purpose hall

In converting the Corn Exchange into a multi-purpose hall, the City of Cambridge, as owner and developer, respected the fact that the building consisted essentially of a great single space, spanned by iron arches supporting a timber roof structure. The building stands in the centre of Cambridge, immediately to the south of the Guildhall. Built in 1875 to the design of a local architect and engineer, R.R. Howe, it has yellow brick walls and large window openings with round, diaper-brick arches and two-light windows with rosettes above. It served not only as a corn exchange but also as a concert hall, from the opening ceremony to the 'Celebrity Subscription Concerts' in the 1920s, which numbered the violinist Fritz Kreisler among the performers. More recently, the corn exchange function having ceased, the building has been used for pop concerts, exhibitions, wrestling, roller-skating and badminton.

The original study for the conversion, undertaken in 1971 shortly after the building was listed, proposed a concert hall with the flexibility to house as many other activities as possible, providing these did not adversely affect the performance of music. Because of the lack of foyer space, most of the yard on the west side of the building was to have been built over. It took another ten years and a revised proposal, which restricted any new building to a small extension at the back of the yard, before a start was made on the conversion.

Above: *The long bar at the back of the raked gallery.*

Right: *The foyer under the raked gallery. Beyond the arched doorway is the entrance lobby, and on the right is one of two staircases and bridges that lead to the stalls and gallery.*

Opposite, above: *The north entrance front of the Corn Exchange, with its tall central chimney, three gables, and round diaper-brick arches over window and door openings.*

Opposite, below: *The multi-purpose hall with its raked gallery and extendable stage. The original iron arches and timber roof structure have been restored.*

The Cambridge Corn Exchange was re-opened at the end of 1986, offering a wide variety of activities, ranging from concerts, opera, ballet and spectator sports like wrestling, boxing and snooker, to roller-skating, motor shows, social events and the annual beer festival. In addition the building is fully equipped for conferences and can accommodate art, industrial and craft exhibitions, as well as the University examinations.

The major work consisted of building a raked gallery structure for 500 seats at the northern end of the hall and forming a foyer with a bar and cafeteria underneath. The stalls, or orchestra area, (which consist of both retractable and removable seating, so that the whole floor can be cleared) together with the three new boxes on the west wall, account for another 950 seats. A fixed stage was built across the full width of the hall at its southern end, and two electrically operated screw-jack lifts were installed to allow the stage to be extended. The stage area is fully equipped with sound, lighting and video projection equipment hung from steel gantries, and behind the stage, dressing-rooms were created out of existing space. Adequate fire-escape routes, an essential requirement of theatres and concert halls, meant inserting a number of steel staircases, one of which emerges in the yard near the street front in an elegant curve, making an acceptable addition of an unavoidable necessity.

Vartiovuori Observatory, Turku, Finland

Observatory into astronomical and maritime museum

Below: *First-floor plan showing the rotunda with a major wing on the north side and two minor wings on the east and west sides. At this level and in the rotunda proper above, virtually all the spaces are for the display of the maritime museum and astronomical collections.*

Bottom: *Section through the major wing, with the rotunda and minor wings behind.*

Below, right: *The entrance hall on the ground floor of the major wing, which also contains the administrative and social facilities.*

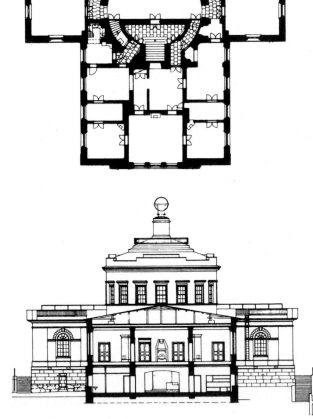

The neo-classical observatory on Vartiovuori Hill overlooking Turku, the former capital of Finland, was built to the designs of Carl Ludwig Engel in 1818–19. A student of Schinkel, the great German neo-classical architect, Engel had been invited to assist in the reconstruction, after a fire in 1808, of the new capital, Helsinki. He ultimately became Controller of Public Works, completing the largest architectural group in the north designed as a single conception: the senate square, senate house and cathedral.

To make astronomical observation easier, but contrary to Engel's wishes, the Turku observatory was built with its rear facing the city. When the observatory in Helsinki was completed in 1834, the equipment was moved there from Turku, thus ending use of the building as an observatory. In 1836 the Turku Seamen's School moved in, and the city took over the building. The School acquired new premises in 1967, and the observatory was left empty, except for the caretaker's apartment.

In 1974 the city council agreed to convert the observatory into a maritime and astronomical museum, and decided that the disused water tank nearby should also be converted into museum space. The plan was prepared in 1977 and the building work began in earnest in 1978. The renovation, carried out by the city, was completed in 1984, and the interior fitting out was executed in 1986–87.

The building is essentially a rotunda with a major wing incorporating the entrance, and two minor wings containing ancillary accommodation. The roofing, windows and some exterior doors were renewed, and the external stucco was repaired. In renewing windows and doors, the old pattern of panes

A suite of exhibition rooms on the first floor of the major wing, showing typical panelled doors and some of the elaborate floor finishes.

and panels was retained. Inside, new electrical and air-conditioning services were introduced to meet the needs of a modern museum, but whenever possible, the surface finishes and details from different periods were preserved. These included the ceiling painting from the 1890s in the semi-circular hall on the first floor; the stucco frieze in the circular hall on the second floor; and some of the floor decoration.

The original room divisions were respected and the new functions fitted into the existing spaces. The administrative and social facilities required by the museum occupy the ground floor. The maritime museum and astronomical collections are housed on the two upper floors, in and around the semi-circular and circular halls; and the old water tank has been turned into storage and temporary exhibition space for the museum.

Left: *The semi-circular exhibition area on the first floor, which lies under the rotunda proper. The perimeter consists of an ambulatory which is glimpsed here through a screen of arches.*

Above: *Light fitting in one of the exhibition rooms, incorporating angled mirrors to direct the light.*

Right: *The rotunda on the second floor, with its flat dome, stucco frieze and marquetry floor beautifully restored.*

Left: *The ambulatory to the semi-circular exhibition area on the first floor.*

Above: *Detail of a showcase. As the building is not air-conditioned, the most sensitive exhibits are protected in hermetically sealed glass cases, in which stable conditions are maintained with silica-gel salt.*

Above right: *A modest flight of steps against the outer wall leads up from the first floor to the rotunda.*

Right: *The entrance to the changing exhibition area in the old water tank, a small separate building that was built at the same time as the observatory.*

Courthouses, Cambridge, USA

Courthouses into offices and arts centre

The two courthouses in east Cambridge, Massachusetts, now converted into offices and an arts centre and facing one another across the newly formed Bulfinch Square, lie at the heart of something larger. The older of the courthouses on the west side of the square, originally designed by Charles Bulfinch in 1814 and enlarged in 1848, faces the old Superior Courthouse built in 1877 and twice enlarged, in 1889 and 1924. A clutter of accretions was removed to reveal the handsome form of the two buildings, and a twentieth-century wing that connected the buildings was demolished to create the square. The Corinthian colonnade, known only from an 1850 lithograph, was rebuilt, forming an entrance porch to the Bulfinch building and emphasizing the north–south axis of the square. This axis runs from the new gazebo at the top of the steps that lead up to the square from Thorndike Street, to the projected amphitheatre opposite the grand portico of the 1896 Registry of Deeds in Otis Street. A cross-axis is planned, running east–west along Otis Street, which will be closed to traffic and landscaped to connect with the new Lechmere Canal Park one block away.

It seems extraordinary that this fine group of solidly constructed red-brick buildings was due to be demolished and replaced by sky-scrapers, one of which – a county courthouse – was in fact built. A scandal connected with this development, however, brought into office in 1974 a new group of county commissioners who cancelled the rest of the development. In 1976 the Preservation Tax Act was passed, and the following year Cambridge established the Multi-Cultural Arts Center, which was in need of a home. In 1979 money for the restoration of the buildings and the creation of Bulfinch

A clutter of accretions, including a twentieth-century wing that connected the two courthouses, was demolished to provide the opportunity of creating a public square and of restoring the façades (opposite, above). This restoration included the reinstatement, on the side of the new square, of Charles Bulfinch's Corinthian colonnade and of the round-headed windows introduced by Alexander Parris in 1848 when he enlarged the courthouse (opposite, below left). The courtroom in the old Superior Courthouse (opposite, below right) can now be used as a theatre or concert room, the gallery surrounding the room providing the lighting platform.

Square became available in the form of a federal Urban Development Action Grant.

The architects, Graham Lund Associates, were also the developers, and they took a risk where no ordinary developer would do so. They look for unusual projects where architecture matters, and as they are prepared to have a longer return on their investment, they spend more money to do the job properly than an ordinary developer would. At Bulfinch Square they themselves took over the Bulfinch building and demonstrated in the sales office how a prospective tenant might furnish the courtrooms without destroying the spaces, by installing an open-plan office system. The intention was that the elegant rooms should become lawyers' offices, but sadly, space has been slow to rent. The Multi-Cultural Arts Center, which provides space and facilities for the many arts groups in the city, occupies the 1889 wing of the old Superior Courthouse, with its studios, galleries, offices and theatre. The last is housed magnificently – but with some difficulty, since the rich plaster decoration and ornate cast-iron balcony are unfortunately obscured by stage lights and curtains – in the finest of the old courtrooms.

When the architect-developers began the work, the interiors had reached an extreme stage of dilapidation. Enough survived, however, for the original plaster mouldings, carved woodwork and paint colours to be meticulously restored. The cupola over the Bulfinch building was re-gilded, the clock mechanism renovated, and the thousand-bell carillon electrified. Externally the buildings have also been carefully restored, with new brick matching the old, and tinted cast concrete matching the old brown stone.

The new square between the two courthouses forms a north–south axis which runs from the gazebo at the foot of the new courthouse (from which the view above was taken) to the grand portico of the 1896 Registry of Deeds. The courtrooms in both buildings (left and right) have elaborate plaster ceilings, stencilled walls, and ornamental railings and light fittings, all of which have been carefully restored.

Les Pâquis School, Geneva, Switzerland

School into public library

One of the first-floor reading rooms, formerly a classroom, with the 'floating' Corinthian column attached to a real column visible through bookshelves on the extreme right. On the left, Pierre Montant's mural painting, an infinite vista of sea and sky, carries over doors and round corners regardless of any divisions.

The old school in the Pâquis quarter of Geneva, a handsome neo-classical building built in 1857 to the designs of Auguste Bourdillon, was threatened with demolition in the city's comprehensive redevelopment project, 'Pâquis-Centre'. After implementing the first phase of this development, the city suddenly changed its mind and decided instead to preserve the school and convert it into a branch library. The work was completed in 1981.

The stucco and stone exterior was restored and the only changes made were to the stonework above the two entrance doors, where the name of the library was carved; and to the roof, where a handful of light dormers in smoked glass indicate a change of use in the attic. One of the entrance doors also serves as an exit to the new escape staircase that was required by fire regulations.

The simple, conventional exterior in no way prepares one for the complexity of the interior, which is due mainly to the addition of a staircase in a glass cage set at 45 degrees to the existing building. This staircase disturbs the simple disposition and geometry of the three basically unaltered principal rooms on each floor, yet provides a strong point of reference and draws attention to the link between the different parts of the library. It extends up to the attic, which has been reclaimed and converted into the children's library by lowering the floor and by insulating and lining the underside of the roof.

A new staircase in a glass cage set at 45 degrees to the existing walls (right) *becomes the centre of attention in an otherwise calm and relatively unaltered interior, stressing the importance of vertical connections between the different parts of the library. The staircase extends up to the attic* (above), *which has been reclaimed and converted into the children's library.*

Two large steps have been provided, on which children can sit and read, in an area that is otherwise unusable because the ceiling slopes down to the floor level.

New openings have been made between the three main rooms on the ground and first floors, providing long views from one end of the building to the other, and revealing the fact that all the wall and ceiling surfaces are uniformly white. Other openings offer peeps through from one floor to the next and reinforce the visual connection already provided by the new staircase. There are also tricks and jokes: mirrors behind glass on the ground floor result in a violent juxtaposition of transparency and reflexion; and on the first floor the 'floating' Corinthian column salvaged from the old building, which is attached to a real column, is seen against an imaginary column in a *trompe-l'oeil* mural.

The conversion has been acclaimed by both the public using the library and the library staff. There is no better proof of this than in the way the interiors have been maintained. The library today looks as pristine and delightful as it did when it was first opened eight years ago.

The control desk on the first floor. Behind it stands one of the original dividing walls, in which openings have been cut to provide long views from one end of the building to the other. The opening on the left is in the shape of a 'P' for Pâquis, and through it can be seen, once again, the 'floating' Corinthian column.

Ground-floor plan (below) *showing how the three principal rooms have remained basically unaltered, and how the new transparent staircase has been inserted in a deliberately disturbing manner. The left-hand entrance door (right), which was used by the girls of the school, now merely serves an escape staircase (see plan). The stucco and stone exterior has been restored, and the only significant additions are the cage-like dormers in the roof.*

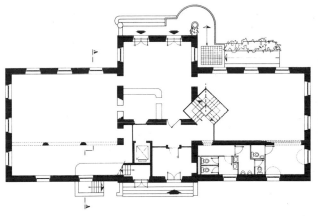

The children's library in the previously unused roof space was formed by lowering the floor, insulating and lining the underside of the roof, and inserting continuous seating in the otherwise unusable angle between ceiling and floor.

Varney School, Manchester, USA

School into housing for the elderly

The formerly unused attic space has been converted into apartments. The central sky-lit atrium, which has been carved out of the existing structure to provide a generous circulation area, rises through the full height of the building. Roof trusses have been left exposed, and blatantly modern details, such as handrails and balustrades, stand in contrast to some of the interior features which have been preserved on the lower floors.

The Varney School, converted since 1983 into 78 apartments for the elderly, stands on a hill overlooking the city of Manchester in New Hampshire. A solid-looking structure of red brick with rusticated stone banding, window-sills and lintels, and a steeply pitched slate roof, it was originally built in 1890, to the designs of F.W. Stickney, as an elementary school. A central feature is the front elevation, which piles exuberantly on top of its great stone entrance arch a corbelled bay and gable carrying a bell tower. Because of the changing demographics of school-age children in Manchester, the school became surplus to the city's requirements after the Second World War and was sold for private redevelopment.

The conversion, which was funded partly by the New Hampshire Housing Finance Agency, included complete exterior restoration and the construction of a new five-storey addition to provide an economically viable number of apartments. This addition is built of the same red brick and slate as the old building, and in a confidently robust manner that makes it at once compatible with the old and unmistakably of its time. The previously unused lower

Above: *The old school from the north-west. The front elevation with its central bay is crowned by an extravagant gable and bell tower. In the distance on the right can be seen the five-storey addition needed to provide an economically viable number of apartments. A view of the atrium at first-floor level (right) shows some of the original cast-iron structure side by side with the new tubular handrails.*

ground floor within the old building now houses the administration, a community room and storage, as well as some apartments. Except for the library, the raised ground floor is entirely made up of apartments, as is the first floor. The previously unused attic space has also been converted into apartments, and the roof has been broken into with dormer windows to allow light to penetrate the new living areas.

Some of the interior details have been preserved, but false ceilings have been inserted over the kitchen and bathroom areas of the apartments. Most fundamental of all is the new sky-lit atrium which has been carved out of the old building to provide a generous and attractive circulation area. (This was possible because of the exceptional depth of the old building.) The new entrances, now at lower ground-floor level, lead from the two sides of the building into this atrium, which is nearer the centre of the whole complex with its new addition. The old main entrance under the great arch on the front elevation and at raised ground-floor level is therefore no longer in use except as an entrance to the library.

The converted school may now be housing some of its early students. What is certain is that the senior citizens residing in the building refer to it as a happy place, citing the spacious atrium, the·varied colours and the comfortable apartments as particularly successful.

Private Buildings

Castle

Palace

Town house

Country house

To convert the service quarters of the Palazzo della Pilotta at Parma into a national gallery of art, a new lightweight metallic structure of bridges, platforms and staircases was inserted but kept detached from the old walls, which were stripped of their plaster to reveal the full beauty of the seventeenth-century brickwork. Along the slender bridge at the back of the Teatro Farnese, statuary is exhibited inside open packing cases turned up on their sides.

The Sonnentheil House (1886–87) in Galveston, Texas, which has become lawyers' offices.

Palaces, grand town houses and large country houses are the private buildings that are most under threat, which is why the more modest house, in the town or in the country, has not been included here. Ordinary houses, especially in central urban areas, are increasingly becoming redundant because of escalating land values. Eighteenth- and nineteenth-century houses also tend to be large and therefore not only expensive to maintain, but unsuited to today's diminishing family unit. But it is a relatively simple matter to find new uses for such houses: when not subdivided into apartments, they can make good professional offices or, if large enough, company headquarters. Institutions, like universities or hospitals, will happily spread into them for administration or teaching, and there are also many examples of conversions into private schools. Terraced town houses are particularly adaptable, as three or four houses can often be knocked into one.

Most of these adaptations do little good to the original buildings, usually causing staircases to be pulled out and front doors to be blocked up, and if too many houses in one area are converted to uses that are daytime only, the whole character of an area can change, because it will be dead at night. An area that has suffered in this way is the East End Historic District in Galveston, Texas, where many of the prosperous late nineteenth-century houses, like the delightful Sonnentheil House by the Galveston architect Nicholas Clayton, have become offices. Houses in the historic centres of European towns, where a good mix of uses still prevails, can often be restored and used in much the same way that they have always been, so helping to retain the vitality and character of the district. A fine corner house in Lindau on Lake Constance, for example, has recently been restored and contains shops at street level, and offices and flats on the upper floors.

If public funds are available, the uses to which the ordinary house can be put need not be commercially viable, and can be of a social, cultural or even political nature. Thus, Milan City Council bought an eighteenth-century house on the Conca del Naviglio, and restored and extended it at the back to make a kindergarten, nursery school and centre for health and social services. In Germany, at Mosbach, a group of sixteenth- and eighteenth-century houses has become an old people's home; at Ansbach a house in the old town has been converted into a shelter for homeless people; and at Koblenz the nineteenth-century Görrehaus has been adapted to cultural uses. The Markiezenhof, a fifteenth-century palace at Bergen op Zoom in the Netherlands, has been converted into a museum and cultural centre with the help of public funds; and in America, the J. M. Evans house at Phoenix, a Queen Anne style residence, has been rehabilitated by the State of Arizona as the offices of the Department of Tourism. Of particular architectural significance is the conversion into an embassy of the magnificent Tassel House in Brussels, which was built in 1892–93 to the designs of the pioneer Art Nouveau architect Victor Horta.

The feature that recurs most frequently in the buildings featured in this chapter is a sequence of fine rooms, none of which should under any circumstances be subdivided. It is a particular characteristic of the town house or palace, and of the country house built in the classical style, where central chimneypieces and the regular disposition of windows, as well as continuous features like cornices, dado, or chair rails and wall panelling, make it virtually impossible to subdivide a room without destroying it. This need not always inhibit conversion to a new use, however, as other, less formal parts of the building can often be adapted to more functional uses.

The Palazzo Grassi in Venice, converted into an art gallery for major exhibitions.

The Colony Club (1907) in New York, converted by Giorgio Cavaglieri into the American Academy of Dramatic Art (1964).

In the case of the Castello di Rivoli near Turin (p. 60), an unfinished early eighteenth-century structure of colossal scale, the fine rooms have been restored while the museum's more utilitarian functions have been accommodated on the lower floors of the earlier and more functional-looking *manica lunga*, or long gallery. Similarly, in the Hôtel Salé in Paris (p. 76) the integrity of the main rooms has been respected by using them as exhibition galleries, while the more mundane activities of the conservation unit, documentation centre, ticket office and bookshop are accommodated either in the attic or in the service wing. In the nineteenth-century palace in Tehran (p. 74), the rooms on the ground floor, where the elaborate decoration had survived intact, have been equipped with free-standing showcases in the middle of the room, leaving the decoration free to make its full effect. All that is left of the Palazzo della Pilotta at Parma (p. 68) are the service quarters, so that, with the exception of the Teatro Farnese and the grand staircase leading up to it, there were no rooms in which the finite quality of both proportion and decoration had to be respected at all costs. There were instead the vast spaces of the stables and hayloft into which it was possible, indeed necessary, to insert new elements of entirely modern design.

Most of the buildings in this chapter have been converted into museums, and it is a fact that the insatiable demand for museums, exhibition galleries and cultural centres generally, due to a change in working patterns that has left people with more leisure time, has helped to give new life to a number of remarkable buildings. Today's trend towards increased leisure activity means that conversions to museum use are not just aesthetically appropriate, but also make good commercial sense. In New York, one of the great Manhattan houses, Carnegie Mansion, has become the Cooper-Hewitt Museum, the Smithsonian Institution's National Museum of Design; in Venice the eighteenth-century Palazzo Grassi on the Grand Canal by Giorgio Massari, has been converted into an art gallery for major exhibitions; and in Galveston, Nicholas Clayton's extraordinary Bishop's House is now maintained as a museum house with much of its original furniture and decoration intact.

Other new uses worthy of note are civic, educational and hotel. At Heraklion in Crete two seventeenth-century town houses from the Venetian period have been combined to provide a city hall, and at Jork in the German Federal Republic, the Grafenhof of 1651 has been converted into a town hall. Similarly, at Segura in Spain, the Cardizabal Palace, formerly a private residence, has become the town hall. In Rome Peruzzi's famous Palazzo Massimo alle Colonne is being gradually restored in a combined effort which involves not only the Italian government and the Massimo family, but also the Kress Foundation of New York and Cornell University, which is already using part of the palace as a school for its students of art and architecture. In New York the Colony Club, an elegant neo-classical building by Stanford White of 1907, now houses the American Academy of Dramatic Art, making use of the massage parlour, built by a previous tenant in the courtyard at the back, for a theatre workshop. A handsome town house in Glasgow, attributed to Robert Adam, a merchant's house in Istanbul and the Litschgi-Haus at Bad Krozingen in Germany have been converted into small hotels, and in each case provide a much-needed facility right in the heart of the old city.

There are many examples of castles and country houses converted into hotels. For more than fifty years the Spanish government has been converting historic buildings, many of them castles, into hotels called *paradores*. With the exception of the Portuguese *pousadas*, the *paradores* are the only example known to me of a long-term government programme of rehabilitation and new use. Yet such a programme could be successfully adopted by any country that combines a growing tourist industry with an architectural heritage of castles and monasteries – France, for example, or Austria, which boasts 427 surviving castles in Lower Austria alone. In the United Kingdom work of a similar kind, though on a far less ambitious scale, has been carried out by the Landmark Trust, a private organization that has converted many large and small historic buildings for holiday use. On the outskirts of York, the eighteenth-century Middlethorpe Hall, by Richard Carr and Thomas Archer, is one example of a country house successfully converted into a hotel.

The United Kingdom has a wealth of fine country houses set in vast parks, most of which were landscaped in the eighteenth century. Many of these large houses can no longer be lived in and maintained by a single family. This chapter includes two examples: Benham Park (p.80) in Berkshire, which has been converted and expanded with new buildings to serve as the headquarters of an international electronics company; and Gunton Hall (p. 82) in Norfolk, which has been divided into a number of separate houses. Kit Martin, the enlightened entrepreneur who converted Gunton, represents one of a number of organizations that are successfully tackling redundancy in country houses. He began with the ruined shell of Dingley Hall in Northamptonshire; he continued first with Gunton and then with Cullen on the Banffshire coast, a Scottish baronial house of 1600 greatly enlarged in mid-Victorian times; and successfully converted Callaly in Northumberland, a fifteenth-century pele-tower buried inside seventeenth- and eighteenth-century extensions and refacings, into twenty houses, cottages and flats. Trained as an architect, Martin plans the conversion and building operation himself, but employs a local architect, who is within easy reach, to detail the scheme and supervise its construction, which is normally carried out by employing direct labour. His method is to work with the existing structural divisions of the building, making as few changes as possible and preserving all original features. He sells the houses and flats mainly to professional people, retired couples and others who come for holidays and weekends from the metropolis. Gardens and grounds are owned through a management company in which the residents hold shares.

If Martin has worked mainly in the east and north, Christopher Buxton and his firm Period and Country Houses have concentrated on the west and south, and have been in the business for much longer. Buxton has converted some fifty country houses, building up his own direct labour force and so substantially cutting costs. He rebuilt the eighteenth-century shell of Shillinglee near Petworth and converted the outbuildings into thirteen houses. He rescued the Jacobean Charlton Park in Wiltshire from certain ruin – though not without cutting up the Long Gallery into three flats – and was able to restore the eighteenth-century Kirtlington Park in Oxfordshire for himself by letting or leasing the stables. At Compton Verney in Warwickshire he financed the scheme initially by the sale of the walled garden for development and subsequently converted the Gibbs stables into cottages and flats. The house itself is to become a hotel, and Buxton has ambitious plans to make it an opera centre in the manner of Glyndebourne in Sussex.

Another organization that has contributed to the rescue of country houses is the national estate agents Humberts. It has been rightly pointed out by SAVE Britain's Heritage that large redundant houses have tended not to be marketed thoroughly, which has narrowed their chances of finding a viable

The ruined shell of Dingley Hall in Northamptonshire has been converted by Kit Martin into a number of separate dwellings.

Charlton Park in Wiltshire, rescued from ruin by Christopher Buxton and converted into apartments.

new use, and it is this gap that Humberts are now filling. In the case of Hill House in Essex, an important sixteenth-century house that was gutted by fire, Humberts put prospective purchasers through a rigorous selection procedure which pared twenty short-listed candidates down to six. Sheffield Park in Sussex, a Grade I listed house by James Wyatt, with a park by Capability Brown and Repton, was sold by Humberts to Period Property Investments, a firm specializing in restoration, for conversion into flats; and Bosworth Park in Leicestershire, a fine William and Mary house and a hospital since 1936, is to be sold with a planning brief that has been agreed with the local authority.

In France there are numerous examples of *châteaux* and *manoirs* that have been converted into hotels. The reception rooms of the private residence translate easily enough, and with the minimum of change, into the reception rooms of the hotel, but the number of bedrooms is usually insufficient to make the hotel a viable proposition. The problem is aggravated, moreover, by the need to provide each bedroom with its own private bathroom or shower. As a consequence, bedrooms tend to be subdivided, outbuildings converted, and sometimes new wings added. Making two or more rooms out of one space is usually possible on the upper floors of the main house or in the outbuildings, as long as there are enough windows, and any attempt to provide more bedrooms should start there, leaving the grand bedrooms on the lower floors with their cornices and chimneypieces intact. New wings are best kept detached from the main house and discreetly sited.

These basic principles are, of course, applicable to all country houses, whether they are being converted into hotels or to other uses. In Germany, Schloss Grosslobming has become an extension to an agricultural college. At Hechingen in Baden-Württemberg, the Neues Schloss, built by the Hohenzollerns in the neo-classical style between 1816 and 1819 and acquired by Prussia in 1850, as Frederick William IV began building a new castle on the site of the Altes Schloss outside the town, has been converted into the headquarters of a bank. Schloss Banz, formerly a celebrated Benedictine abbey rising above the banks of the river Main opposite the pilgrimage church of Vierzehnheiligen in Upper Franconia, nowadays houses an important education centre; and Schloss Aulendorf in Baden-Württemberg, built in 1740 by the Königsegg-Aulendorf family, has been converted into a spa and old people's home by extending the building with a three-storey residential wing, turning the old brewery into sheltered housing, and creating a pump room, restaurant and kitchen out of the main block.

In conclusion, it has to be said that large private houses are off-putting for developers because they appear to impose strict and expensive limitations on change. The examples in this chapter show, however, that with an imaginative and sensitive approach, and sometimes with the help of public funds, all kinds of private buildings can be rendered financially viable and can thus be opened up for a far wider audience to enjoy.

Castello di Rivoli, Turin, Italy

Castle into museum of modern art

Overlooking the Turin plain, the little town of Rivoli nestles into the foothills of the Alps dominated by its outsize castle. The restoration of the castle and its conversion into the Museum of Contemporary Art, carried out between 1979 and 1984 by the Piedmont Region, is part of a vast undertaking to save all the castles and palaces built by the House of Savoy. Rivoli was first occupied by the family for occasional use in the fourteenth century when it was a fortified castle. It became the permanent residence in the sixteenth century when Emmanuele-Philiberto transferred the capital from Chambéry to Turin, and it was his son, Carlo-Emmanuele I, who carried out the first major reconstruction. Further development in the seventeenth century included the *manica lunga*, an art gallery 450 feet (137m) long by 23 feet (7m) wide, which survived both the sack of the castle in 1693 by French troops and the second major reconstruction by Filippo Juvarra for Vittorio-Amedeo II in the early eighteenth century. After the death in 1824 of Vittorio-Emmanuele, Duke of Aosta – the last of the Savoias to carry out substantial works – the castle was first divided into 24 apartments, and from 1861 onwards became army barracks. Ill-use, the bombs of the Second World War and finally abandonment led to the partial collapse of the roof and vaulting, and to a decision in 1978 by the Piedmont Region to restore the castle.

Juvarra's project, which was on the scale of Versailles, made use of the existing castle, doubled it in mirror image, and joined the two halves in a

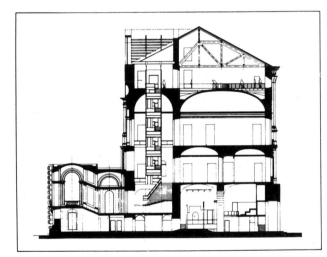

Part of the old castle remodelled by Juvarra in the early eighteenth century (right). *The brick end wall is unfinished because the castle was to have been doubled, in mirror image, and the two halves unified in a grand centrepiece, of which the unfinished lower storeys can be seen on the left. Out of the end wall is cantilevered a belvedere in steel and glass, from which it is possible to enjoy the distant view of the Alps or to admire Juvarra's unfinished plan below. The section through the remodelled castle* (above) *shows the new steel staircase that has been inserted within a vaulted void 80 feet (24m) high. It also indicates the vaulted rooms on the principal floors and shows how the* piano nobile *is here, unusually, on the second floor.*

The new staircase (opposite) *passes through the vault into the converted attic, where it is suspended on steel cables from a concrete lintel. The vault is painted by the Rivoli artist Antonio Carena to resemble blue sky with whispy white clouds.*

grand centrepiece containing a hall three storeys high flanked by monumental staircases. Of all this only some of the remodelling of the existing castle and a mere fragment of the centrepiece, barely up to first-floor level, were ever completed. In restoring the castle it was felt essential to preserve its unfinished character. Vertical circulation had always been inadequate, so a new staircase and lift, free of the surrounding walls and built in steel, were inserted into a vaulted void, prepared at the end of the eighteenth century to receive a grand staircase that was never built. This void, which rises through three floors and is 80 feet (24.5m) high, gives a good idea of the vertical scale of the building, the *piano nobile* alone having a ceiling height of more than 30 feet (9m). The new staircase breaks through the vault to provide access to the top floor and is suspended on two steel cables fixed to a beam in the roof.

Also on the top floor a belvedere in steel and glass has been cantilevered through the unfinished gable end so that visitors may enjoy the distant view of the Alps or admire Juvarra's unfinished plan, visible below in the paving pattern and in the built fragment, the top of which has been protected with beautifully crafted copper capping.

For the inaugural exhibition many artists were invited to create a work for a specific setting within the castle. There have been regular exhibitions since then, but the museum will not be able to function fully until the restoration of the *manica lunga* has been completed. Here will be housed the administration, library, information centre, laboratories and storage for the museum, as well as two spectacular galleries running the whole length of the first and second floors. Because the building is so narrow, it has been found necessary to add to the north side a series of staircase blocks and galleries which, like all the new work, will be constructed of steel, concrete and glass.

Opposite: *The magnificent room with semi-circular corner niches, one of the state rooms on the first floor, was first decorated by Juvarra and has been meticulously restored. Marble for the floor was obtained from the same quarry that supplied the material in the eighteenth century. The room is part of the museum and is used for exhibiting contemporary works of art.*

The built fragment of the central block (right) is now capped with copper sheet for protection against the weather. The arched opening, flanked by columns, marks the entrance to one of two monumental staircases planned on either side of the grand entrance hall but never completed.

Castello Guidi, Vinci, Italy

Castle into museum of Leonardo

The conversion of the castle at Vinci into a museum forms part of a wider plan to rehabilitate a number of sites associated with Leonardo. These include the piazza in front of the castle, with its new paving; Leonardo's birthplace at Anchiano 1¼ miles from Vinci (now exhibiting posters illustrating the various fields of Leonardo's studies, together with blow-ups of his drawings of the Tuscan landscape and quotations about the natural world taken from his fascinating notebooks); and restoration (still under way) of the historic footpath, used for centuries by farmers, which links the house with the town.

The castle dates from the tenth century and belonged to the Counts Guidi. In 1919 it was taken over by the town council and in 1936 a restoration brought it back to its original form – a tall vertical block, appended to an even taller staircase tower, and a lower horizontal block along one side. On the

The newly paved piazza at the foot of the castle (opposite). *In the great hall on the first floor are exhibited machines for movement by land, sea and air* (right). *Suspended from the ceiling is a model of Leonardo's flying machine, and below stands a section of a paddle boat.*

town side a broad flight of ramped steps by the side of the castle wall leads to an inner courtyard, from which there is access to the ground floor or, by means of an outside staircase, to the floor above. On the opposite side the view is to the Tuscan hills, and the ground falls steeply, first to the level of the newly paved piazza and then to the ring road.

The museum was in fact founded in 1953, but the growth in research into Leonardo's work suggested a complete restructuring of the exhibits, which was only completed in 1986. The museum is organized on three levels, Leonardo's parachute hung from the tower marking out the museum from a distance. On the ground floor there is a display of models divided into groups: construction machines, siege engines, clocks, flying devices, bridges etc. On the first floor there is an exhibition of life-size working models of machines for movement by land, sea and air. A staircase inside the tower leads up to the second floor with its lecture room and audio-visual facilities. Here a series of mathematical solids hang from the ceiling, and on the walls are prints of Leonardo's illustrations to the *De Divina Proportione* (1509) by Luca Pacioli. This room contains a video library and is used for showing documentaries of the life, travels and works of Leonardo in his many guises – as artist, scientist and engineer.

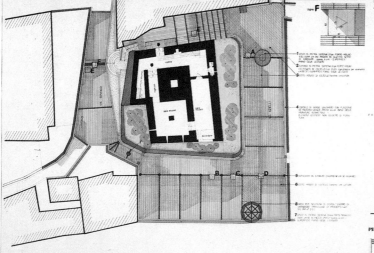

The tall form of the castle (above) *dominates the village and sits firmly on the stone wall which marks the dramatic change in level between the piazza and the road.*

Ground-floor plan showing the castle in its village setting (left). *The piazza is on the right, and the street leading to the castle, on the left. The details on the right of the plan show designs for the brick paving on the piazza and surrounding streets.*

Leonardo's parachute is suspended from the tower over the inner courtyard (opposite), *marking out the museum from a distance.*

Palazzo della Pilotta, Parma, Italy

Farnese palace into art gallery

The Palazzo della Pilotta – pelota was played here under the Bourbons – on the west bank of the river in the centre of Parma, was built in 1583 to house the Farnese dynasty. Continually extended, it became more than a private residence and eventually contained numerous collections, including the National Gallery of Parma, the Palatine Library and the Teatro Farnese, Aleotti's famous early seventeenth-century theatre built of wood, which was seriously damaged during the Second World War but then beautifully restored. After the War the semi-derelict palazzo proper was demolished and only the vast service quarters, which included the theatre, were retained. It is in two wings of these service quarters, with the entrance up the 'imperial' staircase and through the Teatro Farnese (which cannot be used as a theatre because of its wooden construction) that the picture gallery has been installed over the last decade.

After removing insensitive additions, repairing the damage caused by the military and strengthening the structure, a temporary exhibition in the north wing provided the opportunity to develop a display system. Ultimately it was a light, scaffold-like structure that formed the basis for a flexible display framework supporting modular panels that can be used horizontally as floor, or vertically as partition. This structure, combining fine suspension wires and elegant steel handrails, is kept clear of, and stands in sharp contrast to, the surrounding wall structure, which has been stripped of its plaster and gently sand-blasted to reveal the full beauty of the seventeenth-century brickwork.

With such an extended plan, good circulation was an essential requirement. Once inside the theatre, a long, narrow ramp leads on to the stage, the drama

Above: *Part of the service quarters, left after the demolition of the semi-derelict palazzo proper, which would have blocked out most of this view. The car park in the Piazzale della Pace on the right used to be gardens.*

Right: *A detail of the bridge at the back of the Teatro Farnese. The view through the arch is of the stage and auditorium beyond. The free-standing panels support paintings, bas-reliefs and other works of art.*

Opposite: *Sky-lights slit along perimeter walls diffuse natural light on to the paintings. A gap is maintained between the old and new structures. In the gap between the panels and the wall on the left is a staircase which leads to a lower level.*

At the entrance to the north wing (above) *statues perch on a steel beam which is set diagonally across the corner and hung from the existing walls. The visitor enters through the Teatro Farnese* (top) *and up the narrow ramp on to the stage. After the damage suffered in the Second World War the theatre was beautifully restored, except for the ceiling, which was omitted to expose the roof trusses.*

Right: *In the north wing a dense structure of white scaffolding provides support for an additional floor as well as fixing points for panels and lights. Underneath the new staircase can be seen a preserved portion of the old barrel vaulting over the stables.*

being heightened throughout by the exposure of the roof trusses. At the back of the stage, the first exhibition area of large panels supporting works of art makes the visitor change direction and cross a slender bridge into the *piano nobile* of the west wing. Here the space has been divided horizontally with a lightweight floor, which is connected to the lower level by a series of narrow ramps. Staircases at each end of this wing provide means of escape and access to other parts of the building.

At the northern end the route continues to the upper floor of the north wing, which was formerly the hayloft. Parts of the barrel-vaulted floor were found to incorporate brick conduits (conceivably shoots for fodder from the hayloft to the stables below) and these were preserved as evidence of Farnese building technology. To make use of the exceptional height of the north wing, a dense structure of white scaffolding was inserted below the strengthened roof trusses; this provides support for an additional floor as well as fixing points for panels and lights. Wherever possible, the roof has been stripped back and skylights have been fitted along the perimeter of the building, to allow natural light to penetrate the galleries.

Ibrahim Pasha Palace, Istanbul

Palace into national museum

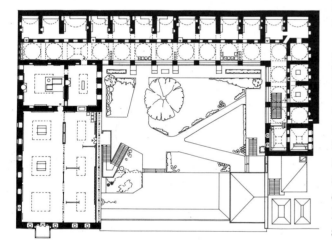

The first-floor plan (above) *shows how the former palace was divided into three segregated areas (for men, women and servants) and how the buildings were arranged around three sides of a court, which remained open on the side of the* maidan. *The palace was built on two levels* (right), *and in its conversion to a museum, the servants' quarters on the ground have become an archive centre and offices, while the men's and women's quarters on the upper, arcaded floor are now museum galleries.*

Situated on the west side of the Sultan Ahmet *maidan* in the heart of Istanbul's historic peninsula, the palace of Ibrahim Pasha was an obvious candidate for conversion into a museum. It stands opposite the seventeenth-century mosque of Sultan Ahmet, the so-called 'Blue' mosque, facing the famous obelisk brought by Theodosius from Karnak in Egypt (AD 390) and placed in the Byzantine Hippodrome, of which the *maidan* forms the southern part. The conversion was carried out by the Ministry of Culture and Tourism and completed in 1983.

Ibrahim Pasha was grand vizier to Suleiman the Magnificent. He built his palace during the first half of the sixteenth century, and today it is one of the few remaining examples of a ministerial residence. Although alterations and neglect had caused the palace serious damage and dilapidation, its original layout had survived. Typically, there were three segregated areas: one for the men, one for the women, and one for the servants. The buildings were arranged around three sides of a court, which remained open on the side of the *maidan*. Within each area a sequence of small rooms gave on to a gallery, which in turn gave on to the central court. The palace was built essentially on two levels, the courtyard level being reserved primarily for services, stables, and storage, while the upper level contained the reception rooms and sleeping quarters. At the front there was in addition a lower level which provided the main entrance from the *maidan*. This level still acts as the public entrance to the museum and has been converted into a ticket office, a reception area and a lecture hall, which has its own entrance from the *maidan*. From the entrance a new staircase leads to the upper floor.

In the conversion of the palace to museum use, the main reception areas on the upper floor have become museum galleries; the servants' quarters, an archive centre; and a nineteenth-century addition, offices. The imperial loggia overlooking the *maidan* has been faithfully restored, with new elements designed in sympathy with, but not in imitation of, the old. These include the grand portico outside the main museum gallery, the roof of which is supported on curved timber members; the outside reinforced concrete staircase, which gives access from the courtyard to the main museum gallery; and the covered way linking the two wings of the palace across the front of the courtyard. This covered way is of timber construction with a roof cover of Roman tiles to match the nineteenth-century addition, of which it forms both an extension and an integral part.

From the public entrance on the maidan *a staircase leads to the vaulted gallery. New elements like the staircase have been designed in sympathy with, but not in imitation of, the sixteenth-century architecture of the palace.*

Qajar Palace, Tehran

Palace into museum of glass and ceramics

A nineteenth-century palace from the Qajar dynasty, standing in the foothills north of Tehran in its own walled garden full of pine trees, has been converted into the city's Museum of Glass and Ceramics. The work was completed in 1978 under the previous political régime, but the revolutionary government of Ayatollah Khomeini has maintained the museum, which has become a popular attraction.

The principal rooms on the ground floor, resplendent with plaster and mirror decoration, marble fireplaces and elaborately carved woodwork, have been restored, and only free-standing showcases introduced. These owe nothing to the style of the rooms but are superbly elegant in their own way, beautifully crafted and technically sophisticated, with an extraordinary repertoire of ingenious lighting systems. The lighting reconciles the new elements with their more traditional setting by combining direct light to the object displayed in the showcase with indirect light to the ceiling and wall surfaces around.

In the other areas, particularly on the upper floor, where the rooms were of less intrinsic interest or had lost their decoration in an earlier conversion, the architect seized the opportunity of creating wholly new spaces by lining the walls and ceilings and integrating the display with this lining. Instead of a contrast between the display cases and their setting, here there is complete harmony and the possibility of viewing the exhibits without competition from their surroundings.

The modest two-storey palace (above) *reveals French classical influence with its octagonal corner pavilions, its horizontal division by plinth, heavily moulded string course and cornice, and its extravagantly ornamented windows and entrance portico. The water basin in front of the palace, on the other hand, is a wholly traditional feature.*

The exploded axonometric drawing (right) *shows the principal rooms on the ground floor, into which only free-standing showcases have been introduced to avoid impinging on the resplendent wall decoration.*

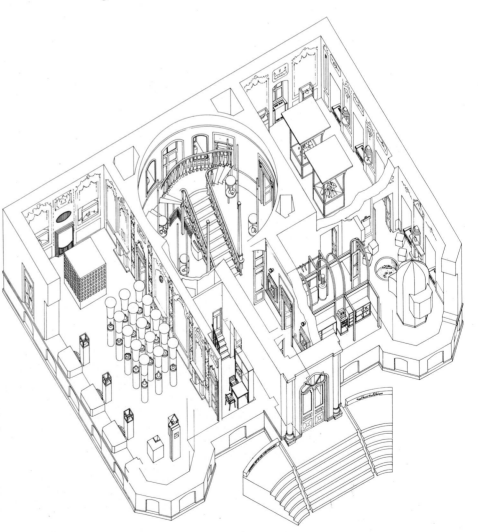

In one of the smaller rooms on the ground floor (top right on the axonometric drawing) two large, free-standing showcases have been introduced. They owe nothing to the style of the room but are superbly elegant in their own way, so that they co-exist quite happily. They also incorporate direct light, which shines on to the object displayed in the showcase, with indirect light, which illuminates the ceiling and surrounding wall surfaces.

No alterations were made to the exterior of the building. Internally, although it proved necessary to strengthen the floors, structural changes were kept to a minimum. The grand central staircase, whose sweeping double curves had previously been boxed in, was opened up and restored to its former splendour. The Viennese architect of the conversion, Hans Hollein, has been called the best interior designer anywhere in the world and a twentieth-century Robert Adam. His own objectives – 'to show the objects to their best advantage; to have light but not to dramatize light; to integrate the old with the new' – have certainly been superbly achieved.

Hôtel Salé, Paris

Town house into Musée Picasso

A large private house in the Marais quarter of Paris, the Hôtel Salé, was acquired by the City of Paris and converted into a national museum to house the art collection that Picasso left to the French state when he died in 1973. The entrance is from the east, through a large portal on the rue Thorigny, into a courtyard, at the end of which stands the main body of the house. A service wing, mainly single-storey and planned around a servants' court, extends along one side of the main courtyard and forms an L-shape with the three-storey house. On the west side the house overlooks a formal garden with terraces and statuary.

The house was begun in 1656 by the salt-farmer Pierre Aubert de Fontenay, who employed Jean Boullier of Bourges as architect, Martin Desjardins as sculptor and the brothers Marsy as stuccoists. Seven years later, when the large house was still unfinished, Aubert fell from favour and had to flee the city. In 1728 Nicolas le Camus embellished the house with wood panelling, doors and wrought iron-work, but most of this and much else was removed at the Revolution. From 1828 to 1884 the Ecole Centrale des Arts et Manufactures occupied the building and carried out a number of damaging alterations. After 1887 the sculptor Henri Vian, who exhibited his work in the house, restored some of the rooms, but also made harmful changes, adding a

The main body of the house stands at the end of a courtyard (right), *one side of which is occupied by a mainly single-storey service wing, its balustraded flat roof now transformed into a terrace accessible to the public. At the top of the grand staircase is a sculpted stone screen* (opposite) *which has been partly filled in.*

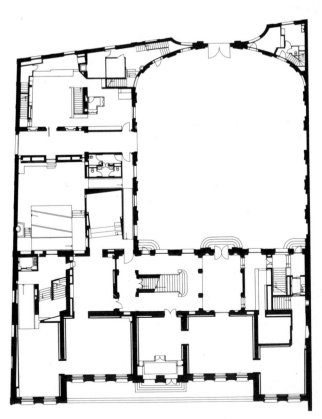

floor over the service wing, for example. From 1944 until 1970 the Ecole des Métiers d'Art occupied the building, causing further damage, especially to the ground floor and basement. The building was listed in 1968 in anticipation of its restoration and new use. In 1976 four architects were invited to submit ideas, and Roland Simounet, who alone satisfied the requirements without adding to the building, was chosen. Building work began in 1983 and the museum was formally opened in September 1985.

The plan of the house is rectangular, with projections at each end of the garden side. The ground and first floors, through which rises the magnificent stone staircase, are given over to the permanent collection, as is the basement, which is reached by a gentle ramp and where the stone vaulting has been exposed and restored. The second floor is for temporary exhibitions and for the reserve collection; and the third floor, which is in the roof space, houses a cinema at its northern end, the conservation unit on the courtyard side, and a conference room, documentation centre and drawings collection on the garden side.

New staircases and lifts have been inserted at the north and south ends of the main building. In addition to the ticket office, the service wing also houses a small auditorium in the basement, a bookshop at ground level, and a flat for the caretaker on the first floor. Clearly, a multitude of services had to be incorporated to fulfil the sophisticated conditions of both security and environmental control required nowadays by museums. It is a measure of the success of the interiors that these services nowhere intrude or compromise a design of great simplicity and beauty.

The permanent collection is displayed on the first floor (opposite, above), on the ground floor, and in the basement (right), where the stone vaulting has been exposed and restored.

The ground-floor plan (opposite, below) shows the main body of the house standing at the end of a formal courtyard with a service wing to one side. Note how the main body of the house is divided longitudinally by a wall, with a sequence of rooms on one side, and the hall and grand staircase on the other. The ticket office and bookshop are in the service wing, and what was once the servants' court has been covered with a glass vault and turned into a sculpture garden.

Benham Park, Newbury, UK

Country house into company headquarters

The new glass and steel roof over the attic well provides a winter garden as well as a meeting room and a circulation route between the various offices at this level. The cast-iron lanterns over the 'tribune' and main staircase have been fully restored.

Benham Park in Berkshire, built in the 1770s to the designs of Henry Holland, was saved from total dereliction by Norsk Data, an expanding electronics company of Norwegian origin, which bought the property in 1983 for its headquarters. The house stands against a densely wooded hillside and overlooks a park landscaped by Holland's father-in-law, Capability Brown. As originally built, the house was only two storeys high, and the south portico of giant Ionic columns was crowned by a pediment. At the turn of the century a large wing was added to the north-east, concealing the stable block on the higher ground; William Nesfield laid out the formal Italian garden north of the house; the original roof of the house was replaced by a full attic storey; and the pediment over the south portico was removed and probably re-used on the north front, which was also built out to enlarge the dining room. Apart from this dining room, which was redecorated in the fashionable manner of the time, the eighteenth-century ornament inside the house was respected.

Lived in until 1939, the house was requisitioned by American troops during the Second World War. After the War it remained empty and fell into disrepair, but it was not put up for sale until 1974, having in the mean time been listed as a Grade II building. Norsk Data, which bought it after nearly a decade of abortive offers, has demolished the Edwardian wing and stable block; restored the original house, together with the later attic storey, and converted it into training rooms and social areas; and built new offices on the site of the stable block. The company intends in due course to restore the Capability Brown landscape and Italian garden.

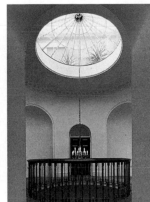

Ground-floor plan (above) *showing the eighteenth-century house in relation to the new development on the site of the old stables. The new offices consist of three pavilion blocks around a central atrium* (top left, *and* right) *from which the eighteenth-century house can be seen. Inside the old house the upper 'tribune' with its lantern has been finely restored* (top right).

The new offices take the form of pavilions, grouped informally in threes and linked by a glazed atrium, which serves as circulating and meeting space. An initial group of three pavilions is now being followed by a second group of three, the six pavilions enclosing an arrival courtyard. The scale and expression of these buildings is comparable with the scale and expression of the former stable block. The forms and materials are simple – concrete columns, glass panels, projecting pitched roofs of slate – and what appear to be two-storey buildings are actually composed of four storeys, with a whole floor of computer installations and storage buried below ground, and the top floor contained within the roof pitch.

The plan of the original house is a series of rooms grouped around a central, top-lit, circular 'tribune' flanked by stairwells, one of which is the grand staircase hall, and the other a service stair. The 'tribune' and staircase hall have lost much of their decorative plasterwork due to damp penetration, but casts were taken, and the plasterwork could always be restored. More serious is the loss of the fine mahogany bookcases that were removed from the niches in the 'tribune', leaving the space unnecessarily barren. The service stair, an uncompromisingly contemporary insertion of white-painted tubular steel with perspex panels and grey studded-rubber treads, has been taken down to the basement, the fine vaulted spaces of which have been converted into a training area with seminar rooms and coffee areas. A covered way, built in a glazed light metal frame, winds its way up the hill to link the old house with the new offices.

Gunton Hall, Cromer, UK

Country house into multiple residential use

A new dining room in the Brettingham house, which has been converted into three substantial houses. This dining room is part of Kit Martin's own house, which stretches the full length of the pedimented south side (opposite, above).

Gunton Hall, a very large Georgian country house a few miles south of Cromer and the Norfolk coast, suffered a long decline until Kit Martin bought it in 1980 and converted it into 21 separate houses, each with its own garden. The house originally formed the centre of a vast estate and looks south over 1800 acres of parkland containing two beautiful lakes. The original block, built to the designs of Matthew Brettingham the Elder, was gutted by fire in 1782 and stood as a ruined shell until Kit Martin reconstructed it. It has pedimented fronts to the east and south, and a west elevation with a central bow. Because of the fire the problem of incorporating grand state rooms did not exist, and it was therefore possible to create three substantial houses, one in the north-west corner, one in the north-east corner and one across the south front, leaving the central section with the bow open to the elements to preserve the romance of the ruin.

Brettingham's house was trebled in size by Samuel Wyatt's additions to the north in the 1780s, making Gunton Hall unusual in that such enlargements normally date from Victorian times. Wyatt's additions included bowed wings with elaborate balconies facing east and west, a fine pilastered front facing east, and a service wing with staff accommodation, kitchen, bakeries, laundries, an audit house, a brewery and a game larder. There was also an attractive stableyard with grooms' cottages of similar date, and a walled garden with gardeners' cottages and extensive greenhouses.

The pedimented south side of the Brettingham house seen from inside, as it had stood gutted by fire since 1782 (above), and after restoration, seen from outside, with the Tuscan colonnade (top). To the north, east and west, the house is encircled by ornamental plantations. The octagonal game larder in the office court (right) has been converted into a two-bedroom house.

Gunton Tower, the lodge at the north end of the park (above, centre), *after restoration and conversion into three houses, with its spectacular flying stair* (above, left). *The Tuscan colonnade on the south side of the Brettingham house* (above, right) *on to which all the main rooms of the new house open. One of these rooms is the kitchen* (opposite), *which occupies what was formerly the west conservatory.*

Before converting the buildings, it was necessary first to improve the drive, to bring a new water main 1½ miles, to install independent drainage systems for each main house and each courtyard group, to provide a proper underground electricity supply and to take down the telephone poles and bury the wires. The construction work itself was carried out by a small team of mainly local bricklayers, carpenters and labourers, together with electrical, plumbing and decorating sub-contractors who came from no further than 5 miles away. The main principle in splitting up the buildings was to make use of existing dividing walls to avoid having to divide any of the principal rooms. All existing elevations were restored unchanged, and the only new structures were small clusters of garages discreetly placed. In the service wing the living accommodation, which had always existed on the first floor, was simply extended downstairs.

The Wyatt wing with the pilastered front has been converted into one large house; the office court, into two four-bedroom houses (the audit house and the L-shaped block east and south of the courtyard), a two-bedroom house (the game larder) and four small cottages (the brewery and the laundry); the Bell Yard on the west side of the Wyatt wing, where the kitchen, bakery and butler's rooms were situated, into four houses; and the stables, into five houses. Gunton Tower, the lodge at the north end of the park, which was in a perilous condition, has been meticulously restored by its owner, Mr Ashley Banks, and converted into three houses for letting, since re-sold and converted into a single spectacular house.

In the five-acre walled garden, where most developers would have built a score of houses, Kit Martin has contented himself with the restoration of the gardeners' accommodation and of the bothy and apple store. The greenhouses with their Victorian vines, which most developers would have simply demolished, are also being restored by being carefully dismantled, repaired and reassembled.

3 Commercial Buildings

Bank

Depot

Market hall

Abattoir

Warehouse

Seaport

Lighthouse

A typical small office in the Kulturmagasinet, a group of four large warehouses in Sundsvall, Sweden, which have been connected and converted into the town museum and library. By leaving the brick walls and heavy timber floor structure exposed, the character of the old warehouse is recalled.

Hay's Dock in Southwark, London, a spur of water off the River Thames, has been filled in, the warehouses on either side have been converted into shops and offices, and the space between is now roofed over with a glazed vault to form a covered shopping mall. The architects were Michael Twigg Brown Associates and the developers, St Martin's Property Company.

Tobacco Dock in London Dock, converted into shops, bars, restaurants and workshops by the Terry Farrell Partnership.

The commercial buildings included in this chapter fall basically into three categories: multi-storey dockside buildings, warehouses and depots with large expanses of continuous open floor area; market halls, abattoirs and other building types that consist principally of a large single volume; and buildings like the Palais Ferstel in Vienna (p. 92) or the Albert Dock Traffic Office in Liverpool (p. 106), which combine large single volumes with conventional cellular structures. When looking for appropriate new uses it is important to understand the characteristics of these categories to avoid converting, say, a market hall to a use that requires the subdivision of its single volume.

Warehouses were originally built for the handling and storage of goods in transit, and they are found mainly near docks, canals and railway sidings. With the decline of commercial transport on the canals, the construction of new docks downstream to accommodate first deep-water steamships and later container vessels, and with the increasing use of road transport, more and more of the old warehouses became redundant. There is no better example than the Port of London, where the redevelopment of the oldest dock, St Katherine's began nearly 20 years ago, and where a government agency, the London Docklands Development Corporation, was established in 1981 to plan and develop the vast remaining area between the London Dock in Wapping and the Royal Docks in Newham. A large number of nineteenth-century warehouses, mainly in Wapping and Rotherhithe, have been converted to a variety of new uses, the most common of which are workshops, offices and apartments. The finest of these, the eighteenth-century West India Dock warehouse on the Isle of Dogs, which was severely damaged by bombs in the Second World War, still awaits restoration and appropriate conversion. In Southwark, Hay's Dock, a spur of water off the River Thames, has been filled in; the six-storey warehouses of 1856 by W. Snooke and H. Stock that surround the three sides of the dock have been converted into shops and offices; and the space between the buildings has been roofed over with a glazed vault to form a covered shopping mall. At London Dock, David Asher Alexander's Tobacco Dock of 1811–14 – a single-storey structure of cast-iron stanchions supporting a timber roof over a brick-vaulted undercroft – has been converted into shops, bars, restaurants and workshops.

Examples of waterside warehouses abound all over the industrial world. They are often very large and splendid – important landmarks on the waterfront or in the city. In Baltimore the regeneration of the waterfront is spreading eastwards to Fells Point, where the gigantic Henderson's Wharf warehouse is being converted into shops, apartments and a hotel with a marina. Another marina is planned close by at Brown's Wharf, where the construction of new buildings and the conversion of a tobacco warehouse of 1820 will provide offices and shops. In Chicago the massive early twentieth-century North Pier Terminal is being converted into shops and showrooms at basement, ground and first-floor level, into offices on the floors above, and into the Chicago Maritime Museum at its eastern lakeside end.

In Bordeaux the Entrepôt Lainé, built in the 1820s by the engineer Claude Deschamps, is another massive warehouse, wrapped around a vast twin nave, seven bays long by four bays wide by two and a half storeys high. It was built with masonry walls and a timber roof structure as the customs warehouse for the port of Bordeaux and occupies an entire island site. Saved from demolition and designated a *monument historique* in 1973, the building is undergoing an ambitious conversion into a 'centre for all the arts', which is now reaching completion. In Göteborg, Sweden, the Sjömagasinet, an

The Entrepôt Lainé at Bordeaux, converted into a 'centre for all the arts' by Valode & Pistre, with interior design by André Putnam.

The Sjömagasinet at Göteborg, converted into a restaurant by Bengt Forser of Forser Arkitekter AB.

all-timber warehouse built for the East India Company in 1775, has been extended to its original length and converted into a restaurant. The decision to make the extension match the surviving original part in appearance is questionable, because it deceives people into believing that the whole structure is original. On the other hand, however, a change, especially to the exterior would have detracted from the unitary character of the building and interrupted the effortless continuity of the elevations.

The great majority of surviving warehouses post-date such timber-built structures as the East India Company warehouse at Göteborg or the Tobacco Dock at London Dock, and tend to be built of fireproof materials. The characteristics of fireproof warehouse construction – thick stone or brick external walls and large, open internal spaces revealing a cast-iron structure of columns and beams – make these buildings eminently adaptable. Perhaps more than any other building type they fit the prescription for new building proposed at the time of the oil crisis in 1973: 'long life, loose fit, low energy'.

Yet there are constraints, and to ignore them will destroy the appearance and character of the original building. The windows of warehouses are usually small and form a regular pattern. A vertical rhythm is established by the crane bays which rise the full height of the building. Internally, there are large open spaces divided into bays by columns and beams, and often by shallow brick vaults between the beams called jack-arches. In a conversion it is important to maintain the window pattern and to refrain from cutting new openings for windows. This means making the plan suit the existing windows – and not the other way round, as is the case with a new building. It is important to respect the structural bay and to subdivide the open spaces as little as possible in the interior. The structural bay of column, beam and jack-arch is so much one that it is better to leave service ducts exposed than to conceal them inside false ceilings and so detract from that unity. In the two Albert Dock examples (pp. 102–107), the suspended ducts are undoubtedly intrusive, but this is a price worth paying to preserve the integrity of the original structure.

The Albert Dock thrived on cargoes from the Far East, India and America until the 1890s, when the new deep-water steamships, for which the relatively shallow dock was inadequate, gradually replaced the square riggers on the trade routes. By 1920 commercial activity had largely ceased and the dock was disused for many years before it finally closed down in 1972. Its importance was recognized in 1952 when it was listed as Britain's largest group of Grade 1 Buildings of Architectural and Historic Interest, and by the designation in 1976 of the Albert Dock Conservation Area. Despite these measures, however, several development proposals were made to demolish the warehouses and fill in the dock basin. One proposal only, to convert the buildings for the use of Liverpool Polytechnic, can be said to have been appropriate and its failure to materialize regrettable.

In 1981 the Albert Dock Company, a subsidiary of a private-sector property development and investment group, formed a partnership with the public Merseyside Development Corporation (set up at the same time as the London Docklands Development Corporation) to regenerate Liverpool's derelict docklands, of which the Albert Dock formed an important part. Having acquired the dock, the Corporation has completed the initial reclamation and restoration work and, in partnership with the Albert Dock Company and with the help of other private-sector partners, has been introducing new uses into the buildings. Dock basins have been dredged and

The Albert Dock in Liverpool, where the Merseyside Development Corporation, together with private-sector partners, has been introducing a variety of new uses into the five blocks of warehouses distributed around the rectangular water basin. These pioneering fireproof structures, in which sugar, cotton and tobacco were stored, were built close to the quayside to enable goods to be unloaded straight from the ships into the buildings.

The Royal Agricultural Hall in Islington, London, now houses the Business Design Centre.

new gates installed to allow watersports and the berthing of sailing vessels. The Albert Dock is now once again a hive of activity based on a great mix of uses, none of which bears any resemblance to the dock's original purpose.

If the safe future of the Albert Dock seemed at one time threatened, that of the Arsenale in Venice, the city's old and now redundant shipyards, still remains in doubt. A recent proposal by Fiat and the Aga Khan for a 1000-yacht marina has been criticized for being too exclusive, despite the extra jobs it would provide. It has been suggested that the scheme might be more acceptable if it were combined with the conversion of some of the buildings to provide cheap accommodation for young people and so supplement the only youth hostel that exists at present. Such a use is also likely to be an appropriate one, since its rough and ready nature would preserve the robust and utilitarian character of the buildings.

Some of the structures in the Arsenale – wet and dry docks, for example – belong to the second category of building types: those that consist principally of a large single volume. The two seventeenth-century salt warehouses that stand on opposite sides of the canal at Cervia, near Ravenna, are divided into compartments, but each cross-wall is pierced by a gigantic central arch with two smaller arches on either side, resulting in a sequence of spaces not unlike that of a church with a nave and two aisles. The conversion of the Magazzino Torre into a place for performances and gatherings, and that of the Magazzino Darsena – a wet dock – into a hall for nautical exhibits is part of a wider urban regeneration project by the architect Giancarlo de Carlo, which includes the construction of new buildings and the reorganization of the piazza to re-establish its central position on the principal routes of the town.

Many of the market halls that survive were built in the second half of the nineteenth century. They are often single-span, cast-iron structures like the two examples included in this chapter: the Schaerbeek market halls in Brussels (p.96) and the Halles de l'Ile in Geneva (p.98). They are sometimes very large; the Royal Agricultural Hall in Islington, London, a cattle market built in 1861–62 to the designs of F. Peck of Maidstone, covers an area of 384 by 217 feet (117 × 66m). Its 150-feet (46m) iron span now houses the Business Design Centre, but it can also be converted into a theatre for dance, as was shown recently when the Kirov Ballet performed there.

The Grande Halle at La Villette in Paris, also built as a cattle market, in 1867 to the designs of Jules de Mérindol, has a smaller central span (90 feet, 27.4m) but covers an even larger area of 780 by 280 feet (238 × 85m). When the abattoirs of La Villette were closed in 1974, the Grande Halle was used temporarily for concerts, fairs and political meetings. In 1982, with the decision by the French Ministry of Culture to convert the abattoirs into a science museum and create the Parc de la Villette, the Grande Halle was given a new lease of life and converted into a multi-purpose hall accommodating dance, music, theatre and exhibitions. The architects were Bernard Reichen and Philippe Robert, pioneers in the re-use of industrial buildings and responsible for another important conversion in Paris, the Pavillon de l'Arsenal (p.112). As a key to the rejuvenation of a whole quarter, Reichen & Robert are at present converting one of the largest spaces of this kind, the last of the great abattoirs built at La Mouche in Lyon, by the engineer Tony Garnier in 1910. This monumental structure of steel portal frames will house exhibitions and fairs; a museum of transport and a cinema for science films; shops and restaurants, all of which will be served by streets; a central square and a sunken forum in the form of an amphitheatre. On an

The Halles Centrales at Lille, which Reichen & Robert have converted into a retail centre of small shops.

altogether smaller scale, Reichen & Robert have converted the Halles Centrales at Lille, an open, cast-iron structure covering 34,000 square feet (3158m²) into a retail centre of small shops. It has meant closing in the sides with shop walls and windows, but the upper part remains open and the walls are sufficiently set back for the cast-iron columns to remain clearly legible.

Unlike abattoirs, wholesale markets, usually separated into meat, fish, and fruit and vegetable markets, tended to be built in a central location. Pressure from rising land values and difficulties of access due to modern traffic conditions has forced many of these markets to move out of the centre, causing the redundancy of many fine structures. The central market halls of Covent Garden in London were converted, like the Halles Centrales at Lille, into a retail centre, but Les Halles in Paris, with the exception of one or two structures that were re-erected elsewhere, were destroyed. In the City of London, the Richard Rogers Partnership has converted the two halls of the former Billingsgate fish market, which was built in 1875 to the designs of Sir Horace Jones, into trading floors for Citicorp International Bank. In Glasgow the wholesale fish market moved out to join the fruit and vegetable market at Blochairn in 1976, leaving the imposing two-tier, cast-iron trading hall, built in the 1870s on the River Clyde and known as the Briggait, threatened with demolition. It was saved as a result of Glasgow's urban regeneration programme and converted into the Briggait Centre, a tall indoor shopping mall with a glass roof and a first-floor gallery. The old fish market near the waterfront in Baltimore is being converted into a centre for night-time activities – bars, restaurants and nightclubs.

Among the third category of buildings, which combine large single volumes with conventional cellular structures, are two transport buildings that have been converted to very different uses. At Rovaniemi in Finland part of a bus garage, built after the Second World War with bricks gathered from the city's ruins, has been converted into a museum of post-War Finnish art; eventually the rest of the garage will also be converted to serve the arts. This is an interesting example of how new life can be given to buildings that have no architectural merit but represent too valuable an investment to be demolished. In Washington the East Capitol Car Barn, a Category II landmark listed in the National Register of Historic Places, stands at the eastern terminus of the abandoned tram system. The main building facing East Capitol Street, which originally housed offices and maintenance facilities when it was built in 1896, has been recycled for residential use. Behind the main building new apartments have been built within the retained exterior walls of the old tram sheds, which have otherwise been demolished.

Finally, it is necessary to mention some examples of commercial buildings that do not fall into any of the above categories. In Galveston, George and Cynthia Mitchell, who were also responsible for the conversion of the neighbouring dry-goods warehouse (p.114), have created a restaurant on the ground floor of Nicholas Clayton's fine Sealy-Hutchings Building of 1895. The rest of the building has been restored and remains in office use. An unusual and interesting conversion is the Sanger-Harris department store in Dallas. Built in 1910 to the designs of Lang and Witchel, the eight-storey steel frame structure was converted in 1966 into a classroom block for El Centro Community College. In Chicago a building that served as the American Furniture Mart from 1924 to 1979 has become what its developer, David L. Paul, has called 'the world's largest multi-use structure', containing a vaulted shopping mall, offices and no less than three apartment blocks.

Palais Ferstel, Vienna

National bank into multiple use

The *Strauchgasse–Herrengasse corner* (below) *with the entrance into the Café Central on the ground floor. The first- and second-floor windows light the former stock exchange hall* (opposite, above). *The Café Central after restoration* (bottom): *it had been subdivided with partitions and used as an archive store.*

The Palais Ferstel in Vienna's inner city is named after its architect, Heinrich Ferstel, who in 1855 at the age of 27 was on a scholarship in Florence when he heard that his scheme had been chosen from among several. His client, the National Bank, had outgrown its premises and had acquired a large site on which to erect not only accommodation for its own use but a shopping arcade, a coffee house and a stock exchange. Ferstel made brilliant use of the irregular site by wrapping the shopping arcade around the two inner sides of the adjacent Hardegg House, leaving the prominent corner of the Strauchgasse and Herrengasse free on the ground floor for the coffee house and on the first floor for the stock exchange. There were entrances to the arcades from each of the three streets, and the three branches met in a lofty hexagonal court with a fountain in the middle, crowned by a glass cupola. Before reaching this point, the Strauchgasse branch passed under an immensely complex ceremonial staircase leading to the stock exchange and opening on to a much larger arcaded court which served as 'outdoor' space to the coffee house. The building was richly decorated with stone and wood carving, mural painting, plaster ornament and marblized stucco in a free adaptation of the Tuscan fourteenth-century style.

The magnificent stock exchange hall with its hammer-beam roof became redundant when the stock exchange had to move to larger premises in 1877, and there followed a series of ill-suited uses. The coffee house, on the other hand, became famous as the Café Central – the meeting ground for artists and writers. The real decline began with the financial collapse after the First World War. The building lost its tenants and by 1945 the Café Central had been partitioned and was being used as an archives store. A total lack of maintenance over many years left the structure in a derelict condition, with the rain everywhere penetrating the building.

The re-planning and search for new uses were helped by the inclusion of the Hardegg House, which filled the corner between the Freyung and Strauchgasse entrances to the arcade. The work took eleven years and was carried out in four stages between 1975 and 1986. It began with the restoration of the narrow Freyung façade and the recovery of the marble hall above the Freyung entrance to the arcade. In 1978 and 1979 the second- and third-floor offices on the Herrengasse were modernized and fully equipped with services, including the provision of a new staircase and lift in the Hardegg House. The council chamber over the marble hall, the second-floor stock exchange *loge* and the four staircases were also restored, and work on the Herrengasse façade was begun. In April 1979 the offices and ceremonial rooms were taken over by two government departments.

During the second stage, from 1979 to 1981, the Freyung branch of the shopping arcade was restored and the shops were modernized and let. The third stage, in 1981–82, saw the restoration of the arcaded court and of the Strauchgasse branch of the arcade. It also saw the construction of a new staircase between the vestibule on the Herrengasse and the coffee house. Work on the Herrengasse façade was completed and the restoration of the last façade on the Strauchgasse was begun. Two new shops were created at street level on the Herrengasse. During the final and most important stage, from 1983 until 1986, the Café Central and the stock exchange were meticulously restored. In each case enough ancillary rooms were included, in the cellar and in the Hardegg House respectively, to enable the Café Central to function as a modern coffee house and the stock exchange as a multi-purpose hall for concerts, lectures, exhibitions, banquets and balls.

Ground-floor plan (right), showing how the L-shaped shopping arcade of the Palais Ferstel wraps around the Hardegg House, which has been incorporated in the restoration and now provides additional space for circulation and services: 1 Café Central; 2 new staircase; 3 foyer; 4 shops; 5 bistro; 6 vestibule; 7 hexagonal court with fountain; 8 Freyung–Herrengasse arcade; 9 Strauchgasse arcade; 10 arcaded court; 11 ceremonial staircase. The former stock exchange hall (above) is now used for concerts, lectures, exhibitions and banquets.

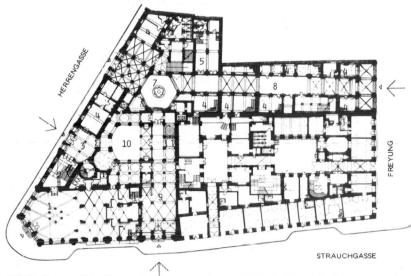

Dairy Depot, London

Depot into design studio and offices

An old dairy depot, now converted into a studio and offices for the design consultancy Pentagram, stands on back-land in a residential area west of Paddington Station. Access from the street is by a narrow lane between houses, and the building, which fills the area left over after subdividing the perimeter into house plots, extends up to the back garden walls of the houses on three of its sides. The old dairy depot, which was built around 1900, contained storage for carts on the ground floor, and on each long side a ramp led to the first floor for the horses. When horse-and-carts stopped being used for deliveries, the building became a warehouse, a manufacturing and printing premises, and was finally left empty and derelict.

When Pentagram acquired the building in the early 1980s they found it in relatively good condition thanks to its structure of cast-iron columns, concrete floors and external brick walls. Only the roof was completely replaced with new steel trusses and skylights. Because of the absence of surrounding open space, side windows were impossible, at least on the ground floor. The entrance front, however, has been given large industrial windows which turn the corner, and one of the ramps has been removed to form an entrance into the building and to allow circulation past these windows. To provide light to the ground floor and, at the same time, the main means of vertical circulation, a large opening has been cut in the first-floor structure and a grand staircase inserted. The same industrial windows used on the outside enclose this opening for fire safety reasons and subdivide the conference rooms on the ground floor.

Other functions on the ground floor are reception, support services and the canteen. Except for a small room at the front, the first floor is entirely taken up with the design studio, which is lit mainly by skylights and provides an exhilarating and beautiful space in which to work.

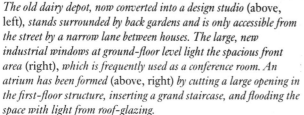

The old dairy depot, now converted into a design studio (above, left), stands surrounded by back gardens and is only accessible from the street by a narrow lane between houses. The large, new industrial windows at ground-floor level light the spacious front area (right), which is frequently used as a conference room. An atrium has been formed (above, right) by cutting a large opening in the first-floor structure, inserting a grand staircase, and flooding the space with light from roof-glazing.

The design studio which takes up most of the first floor. In converting the building the roof was completely replaced with new steel trusses and skylights.

Halles de Schaerbeek, Brussels

Covered market into theatre and multi-purpose hall

The first covered market in Schaerbeek, a suburb of Brussels, was built in 1865. It was destroyed by fire in 1898 and rebuilt three years later to the designs of the architect Jaumot and the engineer Pirotte. It began to fail after the First World War and gradually changed into a warehouse and workshops for the municipal services.

In the early 1970s it was turned into a car park, but already by 1972 a theatre group was rehearsing in the small hall. In 1973, to prevent demolition, the Commission Française de la Culture de l'Agglomération de Bruxelles (CFCAB) undertook to finance the renovation of the market, but it took another ten years for the money to become available and for the first phase of the work to be undertaken. Although the CFCAB bought the building in 1975, cleared the accretions inside the halls the following year and carried out some renovation to the small hall in 1980, it was not until the completion of the first phase of work in 1985 that the old market could properly assume its new role as a cultural centre for theatre, dance, concerts, opera, exhibitions, fairs and circuses.

The building consists of three parts: the large hall on the corner of the rue Royale Sainte-Marie and the rue de la Constitution; the small hall, formerly the fish market, at the back of the large hall and accessible from the rue de la Constitution; and a covered lane with booths down one side, formerly the cheese market, running alongside the large hall and accessible from the rue Royale Sainte-Marie. The *pièce de résistance* is the large hall with its grand

The large hall on the corner of the rue Royale Sainte-Marie and the rue de la Constitution. The exterior has been repaired and cleaned, but the failure to reinstate the arches at the top of the vertical glass panels of the gable has impoverished the façade. The arched doorway on the far right is the entrance to the former cheese market.

structure of iron and cast-iron pointed arches spanning 100 feet (30 m), and its front and side elevations of cast iron and glass. The corners are strongly defined by stone piers and the entrance is a stone pavilion reminiscent of some fragment of a Renaissance merchants' hall. Unfortunately the small arches at the top of the glazed gable above this entrance have been lost in the restoration, and the roof lights in both halls have had to be blocked for performances to be able to take place.

The work of the first phase was of a fundamental nature: new reinforced concrete floors and staircases (the grand staircase at the far end of the large hall had disappeared over the years); comprehensive repairs to the roofs and to the cast-iron and glass walls; the construction of two lavatory blocks; a basic electrical installation and provision against fire. The cast-iron railings to the gallery around the large hall were replaced and extended; the small hall was equipped with lighting and with flexible seating, and a bar was installed behind it.

A second phase of work is planned, which will include the construction, for acoustic reasons, of an inner roof over the large hall, concealing forever the original structure; the provision of lighting, seating and stage equipment to create a theatre in the larger hall for 1200–1500 people; the reclamation and fitting-out of the extensive basement to provide workshops, studios and a store for scenery; and the installation of a permanent heating and ventilation system.

The large hall in use as a theatre, with its roof-lights blocked. Since 1985 the hall has served a multi-functional purpose, which has included concerts, exhibitions and circuses. A second phase of work is intended to provide lighting, stage equipment, and seating for up to 1500 people.

Halles de l'Ile, Geneva, Switzerland

Abattoir into shopping centre

The Halles de l'Ile seen from the Pont de la Couleuvrinière on the right bank of the Rhone. The view shows one of the two parallel wings and the semi-circular block which joins the two wings.

In the heart of Geneva, on a small island in the Rhone, two identical parallel wings, built in 1848 as an abattoir to the designs of J.M. Gignoux, have been converted into a cultural centre. In 1876 a low stable block that prolonged the building was pulled down, and plane trees were planted to create what is now a public square. The space between the two wings was covered with a glass roof, and the building became a food market. This survived until 1969 when new regulations on meat sales forced it to close. At this point the city authorities wanted to demolish the building, and a public consultation exercise merely confirmed that few people wanted it preserved. Nevertheless, in 1971 an architectural competition was held. The winning entry had to be shelved when federal building restrictions were brought in, and it was not until 1978, by which time the climate of opinion had changed in favour of conservation, that the city council voted a substantial sum for the restoration and conversion of the building. The new cultural centre, with its mixture of commercial and artistic uses, was opened in 1981.

It is interesting to note that, at a time when every shopping centre had to have its covered street, the glass roof over the space between the two wings was removed to return the building to its original form. The same space was then excavated to form a basement. The slate roofs of the two wings were renewed, but the stone walls and timber roof trusses were preserved intact. The only extension, built of steel and cantilevered over the river, is to the semi-circular block that joins the two wings at the downstream end. This extension makes the restaurant inside it feel like a boat, with the light endlessly reflecting off the moving water on to its walls and ceilings. Attached to the small restaurant in the main body of the building is a spacious bar and

View from the footbridge which joins the left bank to the island (above). At the far end, the cantilevered form of the restaurant can just be seen. The space between the two wings has been partly covered, and enclosed in steel and glass to serve as an extension to the café (right).

café area, part of which spills out into the space between the wings, wrapped in a steel and glass enclosure.

Elsewhere on the ground floor there are two art galleries, two craft shops and a book shop. On the upper floor, where the circulation is on open galleries connected by a bridge, there are ten artists' studios, a caretaker's flat, and a meeting hall in the semi-circular end block. The centre still awaits completion of the pedestrian routes that will link the bridges and quays to make it the lively place that it deserves to be.

The space between the two wings seen from the bridge which connects the open galleries on the upper floor. At the far end is the steel and glass structure that provides an area with outdoor character for the café.

The new room on the upper floor of the semi-circular block which joins the two wings at the downstream end. Here it is arranged for a conference (above). On the ground floor the café has been extended into the space between the two wings (below).

Albert Dock, Liverpool, UK

Warehouse into Tate Gallery Liverpool

The Albert Dock in Liverpool, designed and built by the engineer Jesse Hartley and opened by Prince Albert in 1846, is the most important surviving group of nineteenth-century warehouses in the world, 'the perfect plaza of water', as James Stirling, the architect of the Tate Gallery conversion, has called it.

The Tate Gallery in Liverpool occupies 129,000 square feet (12,000m^2) of the Albert Dock's largest warehouse, which stands in the north-west corner by the lock through which all ships entering the dock had to pass. In converting the building the architects set out to provide, first, a sequence of galleries for displaying art, with an entrance hall that could also serve as a public meeting place; and, second, the environmental standards necessary for exhibiting art from any collection on the international gallery circuit.

At ground-floor level the existing mezzanine was removed from all areas except the north end, where offices and educational facilities could tolerate minimum floor-to-ceiling heights. This has resulted in exceptionally lofty spaces for the galleries and entrance hall. Also at ground-floor level it was necessary to build a wall to enclose the space behind the colonnade that had been used for unloading the goods from the ships. This wall is opaque, with bright blue and orange panels on the outside, where there are galleries behind; it is made of transparent glass, incorporating a pair of revolving doors, where it encloses the entrance hall; and contains portholes where there are offices, reception and reading rooms at the north end.

A double-curved balcony overlooks the entrance hall and accommodates the bookshop and coffee shop. This new mezzanine is accessible, like all the other floors, by a new central staircase and lifts, part of a service core which also includes the old stair shaft, the goods lift, escape stairs and vertical ducts, and which runs the whole length and rises the full height of the building, passing through the roof to form a cooling tower, water tank room and lift-pulley housing. The service core is contained between two parallel walls, one of which is the old spine wall of the building. It occupies the depth of one bay and divides the building in half, leaving a three-bay depth at the front and back for the galleries.

To avoid the risk of water getting into the galleries, wet plant and incoming services are confined to the basement, while most of the third floor is taken

The section before conversion (below) *shows the mezzanine above quay level and the relatively low ceiling heights that this produced on the lower floors. The section after conversion* (bottom) *shows the mezzanine removed, and a service core inserted, which makes use of the existing spine wall and rises the full height of the building, passing through the roof to form a cooling tower. The lofty attic space has also made it possible to insert an extra floor under the roof. The plan at quay level* (below, right) *shows how the service core runs the full length of the building, dividing it in half and leaving a three-bay depth at the front and back for galleries. The front half at quay level is in fact the entrance hall, which has been closed to the colonnade with a glass wall incorporating a pair of revolving doors.*

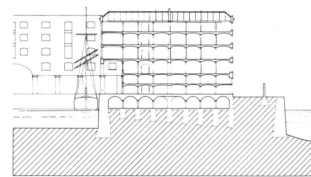

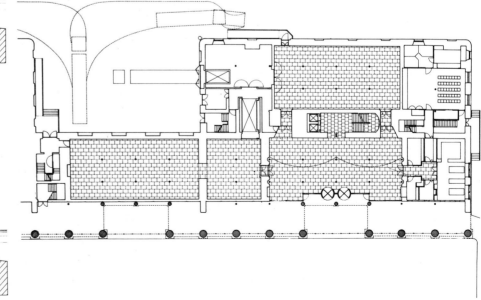

The Tate Gallery in Liverpool occupies the Albert Dock's largest warehouse, standing in the north-west corner by the lock through which all ships entering the dock had to pass (above). The construction is brick walls over a cast-iron colonnade which provides a cloistered walk along the water's edge. The screen wall behind the colonnade is in part-glass and part-opaque panels in bright orange and blue. Inside the entrance hall (right) the same bright blue is carried through to the double bow-fronted balustrade of the mezzanine. Having removed the mezzanine, which extended over the whole building, the architect put back a small section of it to accommodate a shop and café.

A typical upper floor before conversion (above), *showing the construction of cast-iron columns and beams supporting flat brick vaults called jack-arches. One of the upper galleries after conversion* (right) *exhibits Barry Flanagan's 1967 'Four Casb 2', part of the 'Starlit Waters' inaugural exhibition.*

The area at the foot of the staircase in the vaulted basement (opposite) *gives access to the cloakroom and lavatories. Most of the basement is given over to plant and is not accessible to the public.*

over by dry air-conditioning plant which makes use of the existing window openings for intake and exhaust. To achieve horizontal distribution of air and power an inner lining has been added to the walls, leaving a space for concealed services. In the offices, classroom and reading room these wall linings become built-in furniture, while in the galleries they provide the surface on which to hang pictures. In the galleries, too, they mask windows to reduce the daylight factor and to increase the hanging area.

A second phase of construction will convert the remaining upper floors into a warehouse gallery, resident artists' studios, a performance space and a restaurant. Additional galleries and educational facilities will occupy the uncovered south end of the first and second floors.

Phonecards obtainable
from Information Desk

Dock Traffic Office, Liverpool, UK

Traffic office into television studios

The galleried hall of the Dock Traffic Office before conversion (below, left) *and after conversion* (below, right). *It can be transformed into a TV studio, public auditorium, exhibition hall or electronic office, and concealed within the walls and floor are the mechanical and electrical services required for these various purposes. The proportions are double-cube, and there are two levels, with offices off both the ground floor and the gallery. In the conversion the skylight was removed, and the ceiling slightly lowered to accommodate the news studio in the roof space, which was previously a void. The view* bottom, left *shows how well the roof-plane rooms have been concealed behind the restored chimneystacks.*

The Dock Traffic Office, which stands on the north-east corner of the landward entrance to the Albert Dock, is quite unlike the warehouses in shape and structure. With its central atrium, it resembles an early type of office building. Designed by the architect of the Euston Arch, Philip Hardwick, in the form of a classical temple with a Tuscan portico and pediment in cast iron, it was completed in 1847 and enlarged by the addition of an attic storey the following year. Internally, it consisted of a galleried hall of double-cube proportions, with offices leading off it at two levels, and accommodation for the Dock Master. Some 75 clerks worked in the building (roughly the same number as work there now), accounting for all the commerce handled by the dock.

When in 1981 the Merseyside Development Corporation, together with the Albert Dock Company, began restoring the dock, the Dock Traffic Office stood derelict, with the hall full of rubble, its ornate gallery collapsed and the roof open to the sky. The Merseyside Fire Brigade had even been using the shell for training by setting it alight and then dousing the flames and rescuing imaginary victims.

The news studio in the roof space provides Granada TV with one of the most advanced television news centres in Europe. The style of the room reflects its entirely modern function and owes nothing to the style of the Dock Traffic Office, which was designed in the form of a classical temple, with a Tuscan portico and pediment of cast iron.

In 1984 work to underpin the building was begun and the external walls were repaired. At this point Granada TV – a company that had already converted for its own use a barracks at Lancaster and a warehouse at its headquarters in Manchester – acquired the building with the intention of turning it into the most advanced television news centre in Europe. Work on the conservation contract began in March 1985, and the news station became operational in March 1986.

The news studio is located at second-floor level above the main hall, in what was previously a void. (The skylight above the hall was removed, and the ceiling lowered to create the space required to accommodate it.) The form of the space and the associated rooftop plant rooms have been carefully concealed from sight by being placed between and behind the chimney stacks. Other plant is hidden in the basement and in the portico pediment, while a complete electrical sub-station lies buried in front of the building. The central hall and its gallery have been carefully restored, but within the walls and floor of the hall are all the mechanical and electrical services required to transform the space into a TV studio, a public auditorium, an exhibition hall, or an electronic office. The hall can perform any of these functions without affecting the operation of the news centre above.

Kulturmagasinet, Sundsvall, Sweden

Warehouse into cultural centre

View from the south-east showing the two warehouses on the south side, 'Cutter' and 'Sloop'. Both have stuccoed walls with brick bands and arches over the windows. The stucco is painted in different tones of reddish-yellow, and the roof is of reddish-brown steel sheet. The two warehouses on the north side, 'Brig' and 'Schooner' (one of which, 'Schooner', is visible on the right) have yellow brick walls with stucco details. Between the warehouses are the glazed ends to the enclosed streets, one of which, on the south side, forms the entrance to the new museum and library.

The group of four warehouses called Brig, Schooner, Cutter and Sloop, now converted into the civic museum and library, dates from the reconstruction of Sundsvall after the great fire of 1888. (Two other warehouses from this period have also been converted into a bus terminal.) As a centre of the timber trade and Sweden's northernmost port, Sundsvall boasted a large number of timber-built warehouses, which were lost in the fire and replaced by brick structures. The warehouses under discussion were designed to resemble Italian Renaissance palaces by the architects Sven Malm and Gustav Hermansson. The new style was symbolic of the city's successful trading, which had expanded to embrace a great variety of products, from coffee and cocoa to fruit, spices and cereals.

After the Second World War Sundsvall's commercial fortunes declined, and the warehouses came to be used for a variety of new purposes and to be threatened with demolition. By 1979, when the warehouses were finally reprieved, they had been much altered and their condition had deteriorated. The first tasks of the restoration work were to re-roof the buildings, to remove all additions subsequent to the original construction, and to reinforce the wooden pile foundations. Maintaining a constant ground water level to prevent the wooden foundations from drying out and causing the buildings to subside was achieved by building concrete walls to contain the water and by regulating its level with the aid of pumps. The water 'reservoir' so formed could also be used for heat storage.

The cruciform streets between the four warehouses have been covered over with a glass roof to form overflow library and exhibition space, a café and an auditorium, as well as an entrance foyer and circulation areas. This tall, glazed space also collects the heated air from the buildings and either re-circulates it or converts it into hot water. Inside the buildings old staircases and lifts have been removed and new main stairwells built, except in the Schooner and Sloop warehouses, where the existing stairwells have been retained for historical reasons. The main stairwells are connected by bridges that span the covered 'streets'.

The ideal underlying the Culture Warehouses, as they are officially called, was to provide a cultural 'supermarket' that would replace the image of cultural centres as unapproachable places reserved for an élite. Hence the covered street or 'cultural promenade', which retains its character of a public street, and which connects the four warehouses, forming them into one great centre.

The library reading rooms are on the first floor of the 'Brig' warehouse (above), the larger and more open of the two warehouses on the north side. The streets between the warehouses have been covered over with a glass roof (right) to provide an entrance foyer and circulation areas, as well as overflow space for the library and museum.

The new main staircase in the 'Cutter' warehouse (top left) *is designed in an uncompromising modern idiom, appropriate to the character of a warehouse, but without any reference to the style of this particular warehouse. An arched hood moulding over a doorway into the 'Brig' warehouse* (above) *which now gives on to the internal street. In this street at the opposite end to the entrance foyer is a top-lit assembly hall* (left).

Opposite: *Looking eastwards down the internal street between the warehouses 'Schooner' and 'Sloop'. The crossing of the streets is in the foreground, and the café is immediately beyond on the left.*

Pavillon de l'Arsenal, Paris

Warehouse into architectural exhibition centre

The Pavillon de l'Arsenal was built in 1878 as the private gallery of a collector and later became a warehouse. It stands on the boulevard Morland on the southern edge of the Marais quarter of Paris, the great arch of its stone façade reflecting the vaulted form of the interior. It has been converted by the City of Paris into an information, documentation and exhibition centre for town planning and architecture, and it will provide a forum where the public will be able to debate new building developments in the city.

The complex in fact comprises two interconnected buildings: the *pavillon* proper, with its arched iron roof structure over a nave and two galleried aisles, and a conventional multi-storey office block of later date, which gives on to a side street running at right-angles to the boulevard Morland. Together they form an L-shape on plan, and this is most clearly seen on the ground floor, where the main exhibition hall in the *pavillon* extends into the other building and has access from the side street. The two floors immediately above this area contain the offices for the *pavillon*, while the remaining six floors form a separate office block with its own access.

To provide extra space galleries have been inserted at each end at the level of the springing of the major arches and, at a lower level, over the aisles. These new galleries are broken to allow the columns supporting the roof structure to pass through uninterrupted. The glazed arched entrance and the roof lights have been restored, so that the main exhibition hall is again flooded with light. In the adjoining building on the boulevard Morland the rooms at the back have been converted into a conference and meeting room and made accessible from the exhibition hall.

Permanently on show on the ground floor is a spectacular model of Paris, covering an area 25 feet square (7.6 metres square), around which are exhibited photographs, drawings and smaller models illustrating the historical development of the city. At first-floor level there are temporary exhibitions related to Paris or to other large cities, and on the galleries there are topical exhibitions of the latest architectural competition or of developments under construction. It is admirable that the City of Paris should have provided such a centre just when architecture and the environment have become the concern of everyone.

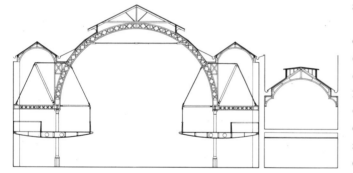

The section through the main exhibition hall (above) *shows the triple-arched iron roof structure over a nave and two aisles. It also shows the new galleries over the aisles suspended on cables from the existing structure. On the right of the main exhibition hall is a separate building which has been converted into a conference and meeting room.*

The glazed arched entrance in the boulevard Morland (right) *reflects the form of the arched iron structure inside. One of the aisles is shown* far right *with its new gallery projecting well into the nave. The structure of the gallery and access staircase is in steel, and the underside of the gallery is in anodized aluminium.*

Opposite: *The main exhibition hall seen from the lower gallery, with one of the upper galleries at the far end. The roof-light and the main structure of columns, tie beams and arches, have been carefully restored. The diagonal boarding on the underside of the vaulted roof was found to be in good condition and has been painted in a very light pink. Floor finishes are oak parquet stained green.*

Dry-goods warehouse, Galveston, USA

Warehouse into luxury hotel

The former Leon H. Blum building (right), *a wholesale dry-goods warehouse which has been converted into a hotel. The façade has been faithfully restored, but, to help with the viability of the hotel, a fourth floor has been added in the form of a mansard roof with dormers.*

Opposite: *The hotel lobby and the atrium that has been carved out of the middle of the building. The floor and wall finishes are predominantly white or off-white, and the effect is appropriately cool.*

Galveston, Texas, is one of several southern US cities where the old warehouses and commercial buildings are being converted to new uses as part of a wider urban regeneration programme. Between the port and the towers of downtown runs The Strand and its adjacent area of dignified and solidly constructed nineteenth-century buildings that survived the Great Galveston Storm of 1900. The area has been designated a National Historic Landmark, and an action plan prepared in 1975 by architects and planners Venturi and Rauch, covering everything from signage to traffic control and parking demands, has largely been implemented.

Of the many buildings for which new uses have been found, one of the most important is the 1879 Leon and H. Blum building, a wholesale dry-goods warehouse with a Second Empire exterior in stucco imitating stone. It has been converted into the Tremont House Hotel by George Mitchell, chairman of Houston's Mitchell Energy and Development. The conversion into a small (125-bedroom) luxury hotel has been accomplished with an eye on the past, with discretion and taste. The hotel rooms have 14-feet-high (4.3 m) ceilings, hardwood floors, ceiling fans and brass

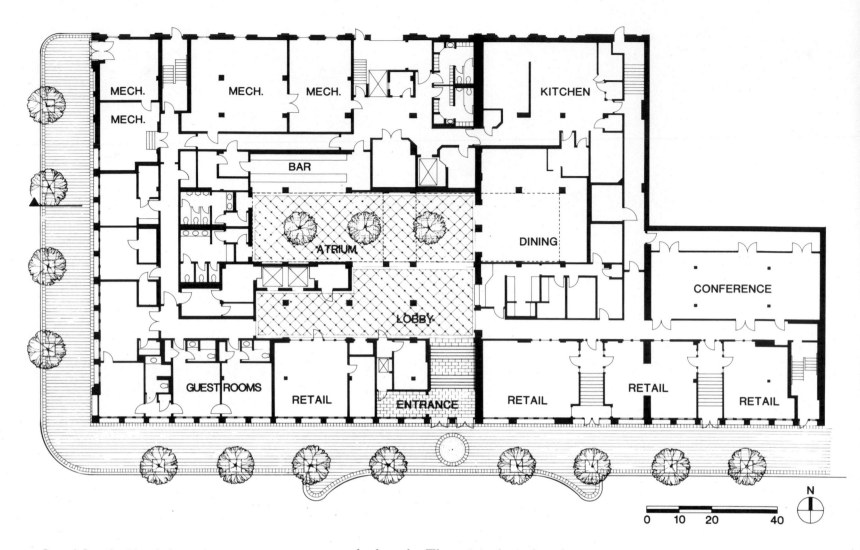

Ground-floor plan (above) showing how a section has been carved out of the middle of the building to form an atrium with lobby and bar at ground-floor level. The atrium (opposite) rises the full height of the building and is crowned for its full length by a skylight.

bedsteads. The original window frames and sashes have been restored, and on the ground floor the arcade has been filled with wood-and-glass panels that match the original pairs of glazed doors.

The most radical change to the structure has been to cut a whole section out of the middle of the building to form an atrium, off which at ground-floor level are the hotel lobby, dining room, bar and shops. The atrium rises through the full height of the building and is crowned by a skylight. Hotel rooms open on to the atrium with French windows and iron balconies, and bridges cross it at the upper three floors to provide connections between the different parts of the hotel.

To help with the viability of the hotel an extra floor has been added in the form of a mansard roof with dormers. The steep slope of this roof, much steeper than the original hipped roof, makes it too assertive and has to be regretted on aesthetic grounds alone. The use of the building as a hotel, however, would not have been possible without it. The hotel's viability, moreover, has to be seen in connection with two adjacent historic buildings, one of which has been converted into a restaurant and a ballroom, and the other into a hotel with conference facilities.

South Street Seaport, New York

Commercial port into multiple use

The Pier 17 pavilion (above *and* opposite) *is a new building made of steel and glass which made the restoration programme a viable proposition. It is a grand, three-storey shed surrounded by arcades and balconies to give the shops and restaurants in the building maximum waterfront exposure and view; and to enable the public to stroll around the building without having to enter it.*

The seaport area in lower Manhattan, built on reclaimed land in the second half of the eighteenth century, was originally the centre of New York's maritime trade, with the first Fulton Market opened in 1822 as an emporium for dry goods. After the Civil War, as steamships replaced clippers and trade shifted to the deep-water piers on the Hudson River, the area became the centre of a wholesale fish industry, with its headquarters in the Tin Building and an overflow of street-level stalls across South Street, in part of the Fulton Market. In the recent regeneration of the area as a shopping centre and museum this wholesale activity has been retained, and the new Fulton Market built to incorporate the fish stalls on its South Street side.

The South Street Seaport Museum was founded in 1967 in reaction to the Manhattan building boom, which was threatening the area. The Museum formed a collection of old ships, which increased its membership to ten thousand and annual visitors to one million. The area was designated a New York City Landmark and included in the National Register of Historic Places. With insufficient resources to undertake major restoration and development, however, the Museum turned in 1976 to the Rouse Company, which had already successfully converted the Faneuil Hall market area in Boston. The result was the 1980 Seaport Development Plan, which was eventually realized with the help of a $20½ million grant for improvements to the infrastructure of the area and the construction of a new pier platform.

The Fulton Market of 1883 (above) *before its demolition in 1951. It has been replaced by the new Fulton Market* (below, *and* opposite, above) *which contains cafés, restaurants and food stalls, and incorporates the fish-market stalls which established themselves on the site soon after the demolition of the old market.*

The plan comprised the cluster of eighteenth- and nineteenth-century commercial buildings now known as the Museum Block; the new Fulton Market, containing cafés, restaurants and food stalls, and incorporating the existing fish-market stalls on the ground floor; the existing wholesale fish market in the Tin Building (built 1907), of which the market stalls on the opposite side of South Street were a part; restoration of the state-owned block of counting houses built by Peter Schermerhorn in 1811 on the south side of Fulton Street; the adaptation of Piers 16 and 18 for outdoor museum functions; and the construction of Pier 17 for retail and restaurant use, and of the 34-storey Seaport Plaza, a privately owned office tower with two levels of shops at its base. The Museum Block houses the exhibition space, administrative offices, library and laboratory of the museum, as well as shops and offices for renting. The new building on the corner of Fulton Street and Front Street was designed to recall, if not imitate, an 1848 cast-iron façade by James Bogardus which would have been re-erected there if it had not been stolen. This is in contrast to the new Fulton Market and Pier 17, where a different firm of architects has deliberately avoided historical references. Yet these buildings, according to an American critic, sit in their neighbourhood as if they had always been there, without donning a costume of any kind.

Fulton Street has been made into a pedestrian area and serves as the primary circulation spine, linking Wall Street and the surrounding business district with South Street and, under the elevated expressway, with the waterfront, where the tall ships and Pier 17 act as a magnet. In fact, it was Pier 17, with its three floors of shops, cafés and restaurants, that provided the developer with the space needed to make the scheme financially viable. The base of retail income will provide the Museum with long-term support for its ships, galleries, exhibitions and educational activities, and will enable it to restore and convert another group of old commercial buildings north-east of Beekman Street to retail, restaurant, office and museum use.

The new Fulton Market, with the corner of the Bogardus building (above). Both buildings have deeply projecting canopies at first-floor level.

The river end of Pier 17 (right) is modelled on Victorian recreation piers and contains speciality shops and restaurants. Its perimeter consists of open decks linked by staircases, from which views across the East River can be enjoyed.

Above: *The museum block in Front Street, from underneath the Fulton Market canopy. This is a cluster of eighteenth- and nineteenth-century commercial buildings which have been converted mainly into shops and offices, but also into a museum, complete with storage, a library and a curatorial laboratory.*

Right: *The 1811 Schermerhorn Row, a state-owned block of counting houses, opposite the new Fulton market in Fulton Street.*

Opposite: *View from Fulton Street of the new Fulton Market. The corrugated steel canopy and the recessed roof-line make the building look smaller than it really is, giving the impression of a two-storey structure of almost domestic scale. A glass strip, where the canopy meets the wall, allows daylight to reach mezzanine windows under the canopy and night lighting to penetrate upwards and light the walls.*

East Brother lighthouse, San Francisco Bay, USA

Lighthouse into guesthouse

The East Brother lighthouse looks more like an ornate seaside villa than a typical lighthouse. The change from a functioning station with residential accommodation for the keeper to a living museum incorporating a bed-and-breakfast inn constitutes only a minor change in use, but the special qualities of the lighthouse, together with the remarkable enterprise that brought about the restoration of the station as a whole, justify its inclusion.

East Brother is one of two tiny islands – no more than three-quarters of an acre in area – on the east side of San Pablo Strait, which connects San Francisco Bay with San Pablo Bay. It was built in 1873–74 by the federal government to guide ships at night or in fog past the many rocky islands and shoals. The lighthouse, situated at the western end of the island, was of timber construction and consisted of a six-room dwelling with an attached tower for the light. The design, which was rich in gingerbread and scrollwork, incorporated a porch and balcony, deeply overhanging roofs and a virtuoso display of sawn banisters. Also built at that time were water tanks, a cistern and rain catchment basin, a fog-signal building, workshop, boathouse and wharf.

In 1967 the Coast Guard wanted to automate the station to save on salaries and maintenance costs. An automatic beacon was installed in the lighthouse, and the last resident keeper left the island, making way for rotating crews of coast-guardsmen. In 1971, threatened with demolition, the station was placed on the National Register of Historic Places. This prevented demolition but did nothing to help maintain the buildings, the Coast Guard's budget only

The lighthouse with its elaborate timber construction fully restored. Unlike lighthouses generally, the building consists of a six-room dwelling with an attached tower for the light. In the foreground is the dome marking the position of the underground cistern, surrounded by a rainshed area of concrete.

providing for the upkeep of the navigational equipment. In 1979 a non-profit-making organization was formed to restore the station and make it available for public use. The same year the Coast Guard issued the organization with a 20-year renewable lease of the island at no cost. Private donations and a Maritime Preservation Matching Grant from the US Department of the Interior, as well as over 300 volunteers, enabled all the island structures to be restored and opened to the public within a year.

In the course of restoration it was found that the buildings were for the most part structurally sound. Only the south side of the lighthouse needed new studs and sheathing, and a new foundation had to be constructed under part of the dwelling. The work included re-instating the sawn banisters of the outside stairs and balcony, and removing the asbestos shingles on the outside walls, which had replaced the original Victorian trim in an attempt at so-called modernization. For the more skilled there were such tasks as reconstructing the ornate woodwork or making and painting the 250 new pickets needed to repair the fence that girdles the island. For the third time in the station's history the rainshed had to be replaced, and this involved taking up the old concrete pavement and pouring 9000 square feet (835 m^2) of new concrete.

Today the East Brother station holds reminders of several periods. The buildings are much as they were in 1874, while the lighthouse floor plan reflects the remodelling carried out shortly after the turn of the century. The fog-signal equipment dates from the 1930s and 1940s – and there is now an innkeeper instead of a lighthouse-keeper.

The western end of East Brother Island with its lighthouse and, just visible on the right, the roof of the fog-signal building at the eastern end.

4 Industrial Buildings

Mill

Brewery

Industrial plant

Factory

An old leatherworks near St Pancras Station in London, which has been converted into a furniture showroom and offices. What used to be a single-storey shed now provides space for the display of office furniture. At either end of this space, pairs of columns, which are cast in plaster and painted, frame a mural at one end and, seen here, a view through to the octagonal showroom at the other.

All the buildings illustrated in this chapter – whether an eighteenth-century flour mill, a nineteenth-century brewery or a twentieth-century factory – share one common characteristic: large open spaces divided into bays by columns and beams. It is a characteristic also found in the warehouse type of commercial buildings, to which attention has been fully drawn in the previous section. In the eighteenth and early nineteenth centuries the structure nearly always consisted of cast-iron columns, timber floors and timber, brick or stone walls. In the early nineteenth century a fireproof construction was developed which consisted of cast-iron columns and beams carrying shallow brick vaults; and in the twentieth century the cast-iron columns and beams were replaced by steel, and later also by reinforced concrete. The earliest example shown here, New Mills at Wotton-under-Edge in Gloucestershire (p.148), dates from 1790 and is a structure of cast-iron columns, timber floors and brick external walls. The most recent example, which dates from 1944, is the asphalt plant on the East River Drive in New York (p.156) with its pioneering structure of parabolic prefabricated steel trusses.

The great nineteenth-century textile mills in England and Scotland represent a particularly difficult problem because of their immense size. There is no better example than the Dean Clough Mills at Halifax, Yorkshire, which originated in a small mill by the River Hebble in 1803. Between 1841 and 1869 eight large mills, from six to ten storeys high, a number of storage sheds and a dye works were built. Twenty-eight boilers and seven beam engines, consuming 27,000 tons of coal a year, discharged their smoke through a forest of tall mill chimneys, casting a dark shadow over the whole of Halifax. In their heyday nearly 6000 people were employed by the mills, but by late 1974 this had dropped to below 2000. In 1982, when unemployment was at its worst, the mills were closed and sold to Mr Ernest Hall, who rejected the options of demolition and redevelopment, or of leasing the buildings through estate agents and, instead, set out 'to create an environment which would deliberately stimulate and encourage enterprise, and thereby form a model for long-term success in a much broader arena. With an astonishing swiftness Dean Clough took on a new lease of life as a wholly integrated industrial, educational and cultural community.' Of the surviving 1.25 million square feet (116,117m²) – one eight-storey mill was demolished in 1986 – 700,000 square feet (65,000m²) are again in use, occupied by some 200 businesses giving employment to 2500 people. The emphasis is on craft, design, fine arts and education. Printers, carpenters, photographers, architects and interior, graphic and product designers have set up businesses, and there is still an element of textile manufacture. Facilities include a travel agency, bank, post office, paper shop, hairdresser, day nursery, sandwich bar and restaurant, and the complex as a whole collects works of art and supports an exhibition gallery and an artist in residence. Most significant of all is the presence of a job club for employment, a local business enterprise agency and an enterprise campus offering technological training.

The origins of Ebley Mill near Stroud in Gloucestershire are much older, a mill a little to the north of the present buildings being first mentioned in 1393. Initially, it was a corn mill, but fulling of wool may have begun here early on, as local entrepreneurs began processing Cotswold wool into cloth instead of exporting raw bales to Flanders. A fulling mill is definitely recorded from 1469 onwards, and fulling and corn-grinding went on side-by-side throughout the sixteenth, seventeenth and eighteenth centuries. It was not until the completion of the Stroud-water Canal in 1779, which gave the mill the

Ebley Mill near Stroud in Gloucestershire, which has been converted by Niall Phillips Associates into local government offices.

advantage of cheap transport, that it became possible to realize the full potential of the site. All the processes of the woollen industry – fulling, teasing, spinning, dyeing and weaving – had begun to move from scattered cottage units and to be concentrated in one large factory block. Three mills, of which one was demolished in 1965, were built in the first twenty years of the nineteenth century, the form of construction being Cotswold stone and timber framing. The long machine shops were lit by two-light mullioned windows with segmental heads, a local form of fenestration which could be found in the neighbouring mill-owner's house, the sixteenth-century Ebley Court, now also demolished. Steam power and a beam engine were only added in 1862 and, in order to accommodate these, the last of the mill blocks was extended with a massive square block and a clock tower reminiscent of a French château, by one of the great Victorian ecclesiastical architects, George Frederick Bodley. This mill has been empty since 1981 and it is to the great credit of Stroud District Council that it acquired the building in 1983 and commissioned Niall Phillips Associates, the architects who carried out the conversion of New Mills at Wotton-under-Edge, to convert the building into council offices.

In France the architects who have pioneered the re-use of industrial buildings are Bernard Reichen and Philippe Robert. Three examples of converted textile mills, all sponsored by public authorities, give an indication of the scale and quality of their work. The Filature Leblan at Lille is a conversion to mixed use, like that of the Wehrli flour mill near Zurich (p.140). The conversion of the Filature Leblan was completed in 1980 and includes 100 apartments, offices, shops, a public library, a multi-purpose hall and a church. At Elbeuf in the département of Seine Maritime, the Etablissement Blin et Blin, a very large group of factory buildings in two colours of brick, has been similarly converted to include small businesses and craft workshops; and at Tourcoing near Lille, the Usine M.C.R. Prouvost has been converted into 162 apartments with space standards that exceed the norms by 25 per cent, a bonus that can often be achieved without appreciable extra cost when adapting old buildings.

In San Antonio, Texas, the magnificent pile of the Pioneer Flour Mills, towering over the charming miller's house, is still functioning as a flour mill. Only the miller's house, known as the Guenther House after the family which owns the mill, has been converted into a museum and tea shop. On the Guidecca in Venice, however, the prominent Molino Stucky, a vast flour mill of 1884, has stood empty for many years and has been the subject of an ideas competition and a number of proposals for conversion. The most recent of these is for 100 apartments, a hotel, a conference centre and a museum, all of which would provide badly needed employment for 500 people.

In Küttingen in Switzerland an early paper mill that looks more like a château than an industrial building has had a chequered history. Built in 1824, it suffered from a lack of water and was forced to close after only 20 years. It became a successful silk factory and was enlarged later in the century. Used as a warehouse in recent years, it was eventually listed as a building of architectural merit and converted in 1982 into apartments and studios, a use for which it is eminently suited, not least because of its beautiful situation commanding a valley. In the St Alban-Tal quarter of Basle, another old centre of the paper industry and now a protected zone of the old city, a very plain mid-nineteenth-century, half-timbered structure over a masonry base, which was used for drying paper on its two upper floors and for workers'

An early twentieth-century workshop at the naval barracks in Helsinki has become the main centre of the Katajanokka primary school. The architect of the conversion was Vilhelm Helander.

The torpedo factory at Alexandria, Virginia, which Washington architects Keyes, Condon and Florance have converted into an arts centre with studios for artists and craftsmen. The building on the right, also part of the naval munitions factory complex, has been transformed from a reinforced concrete industrial building into a red-brick office block.

living accommodation and workshops on its two lower floors, has been converted into apartments and studios. To reinforce the light timber floor structure, two longitudinal beams were substituted for the single central longitudinal beam, thus reducing the floor span of the transverse joists. Otherwise the old structure was retained, and the exposed half-timbering faced with vertical boarding.

At the Merikasarmi (naval barracks) in Helsinki, a major work of Carl Ludwig Engel, principal architect of the neo-classical city centre, several buildings have been converted into a primary school, kindergarten, day-care centre and club rooms. Engel built the barracks between 1810 and 1830, but already by 1844 Engel's successor, E. B. Lohrmann, had made plans for new buildings west of the barracks area. One of these, the manège, or riding school, has been converted into a gymnasium, which also serves as an assembly hall for the primary school. More remarkable, however, is the transformation of an early twentieth-century engineering workshop, a pioneering reinforced concrete structure with a glass lantern, which was built between the manège and an older workshop, also dating from 1844. Originally completely open, the two-storey interior, now divided into a central hall with classrooms at the sides, has become the main centre of the school's activities. A new glass roof, similar to the old one, lights the hall; a system of low shelving is used to separate group work from library facilities; and at each end a new staircase leads to a reading gallery.

Two of the most interesting and unusual conversions of industrial buildings are in America. In Alexandria, Virginia, a torpedo factory built hurriedly in the last year of the First World War and an early example of reinforced concrete flat-slab construction, has been converted into an arts centre with studios for some 200 artists and craftsmen, who can be observed at work by the general public through large windows. The waterfront in Alexandria used to be largely industrial and was dominated by the torpedo factory and a naval munitions plant built in 1943. With the decline of the munitions industry after the war, the area became dilapidated until the city of Alexandria bought the factories from the federal government in 1970. A group of artists and craftsmen were permitted to use two of the buildings as studios so that they could prepare for a bicentennial show. The arts centre flourished, drawing thousands of visitors and tourists, and in 1978 a design competition for the redevelopment of the factories resulted in a proposal to convert the munitions plant into offices and to make permanent the use that the torpedo factory had already acquired. The interior of the torpedo factory was gutted and reconstructed with a new mezzanine level, retaining its industrial character by forming partitions out of standard galvanized metal with glass panels for windows, and by leaving all mechanical, electrical and structural elements exposed.

Even more striking is the conversion in the East End of Dallas, Texas, of a group of grain silos, built to the designs of Eugene Davis in 1946 for the manufacturing and storing of corn chips. So far only a small part of the whole has been converted by the architects Phillips and Ryburn into a design studio for themselves. There is a proposal to convert the remainder into a restaurant and the silos proper into apartments, but the drawings suggest that the latter conversion would alter the silos beyond all recognition and make them look no different from a high-rise apartment block.

There has been much talk of converting the vast Fiat-Lingotto factory in Turin, which has been described as one of the most important examples of industrial architecture of the twentieth century, and perhaps Italy's greatest contribution to modern architecture. The plant, which includes the factory with the famous spiral ramps leading to the test-track on the roof, was built between 1916 and 1926 to the designs of the architect Giacomo Matte-Trucco. It was constructed in largely exposed reinforced concrete to a modular plan consisting of three major elements, which could be used in combination to permit infinite extensions and variations. Latterly it contained only the bodywork shops, because the weight of the new machinery used in mechanical shops had become too great for its structure. Its inevitable closure in the late 1970s led to an architectural competition in 1984, in which some of the world's leading architects took part. A consortium including Fiat later appointed Renzo Piano, who was the architect – together with Richard Rogers – of the Centre Pompidou in Paris, to prepare plans for the conversion of the plant into a hotel and conference centre, an exhibition centre, offices and faculties for the university. So far only part of the ground floor of the factory building has been modified and a column-free hall erected at the back to house a motor show. Renzo Piano has already demonstrated the potential of large, redundant industrial plants in his conversion to offices and public gardens of the Schlumberger works in the Paris suburb of Montrouge. The successful conversion to new uses of the much larger Lingotto works, a conversion that would have to respect the integrity of the spiral ramps and roof test-track, would indeed be his crowning achievement.

Finally, electrical power stations with their turbine halls and to a lesser degree water pumping stations, invariably landmarks because of their great size and distinctive silhouette, pose very particular problems when they become redundant. There are no examples of power stations in this chapter, because I am not aware of any fully successful conversion. However, in Milwaukee, Wisconsin, the conversion to house the local repertory theatre of two riverside power stations belonging to Wisconsin Electric Power has won awards for its architect, Robert Breckley; and in Brussels the Centrale Electrique in the rue de l'Ermitage has been converted into offices which include the Foundation for Architecture. In London Mr John Broom, the developer who is bravely converting Battersea Power Station into an amusement park, may have learnt a few lessons from the waterfront power plant in Baltimore, which was similarly converted in 1985 but failed after two years, despite the successful regeneration of the harbour area as a whole. The Turtle Creek Pump Station in Dallas, the oldest public building in Dallas, was built in 1909 to the designs of C. A. Gill, a prominent local architect. It became redundant as early as 1930 and housed various functions of the Dallas Water Utilities until 1957, when road-widening caused portions of the south and west walls to be destroyed. In 1981, after 27 years of neglect, the building was designated a Historic Landmark, and a committee was formed to find a way of preserving it and putting it once again to good use. The public was asked to make suggestions, one of which, by Mr Jo Jagoda, President of the Greater Dallas Youth Orchestra, was accepted. He proposed converting the building into a rehearsal hall and performance centre for the city's smaller arts organizations – a sort of arts 'incubator'. It took seven years to raise the required 2.2 million dollars and to convert the building, which opened its doors as the Sammons Center for the Arts in February 1988. The conversion retains the original industrial character of the interior, although the original south entrance façade has been painstakingly reconstructed on the north side, and is a model of its kind.

In Dallas, the architects Phillips and Ryburn are converting a group of grain silos into apartments and a restaurant. They have already successfully converted the low building at the foot of the silos into a design studio for themselves.

Lowell Mills and Boott Mills, Lowell, USA

Textile mills into multiple use

The conversion of the Lowell Manufacturing Company's mills, re-named Market Mills, was the first large project to be undertaken by the Lowell Historic Preservation Commission (LHPC) and a private developer, Market Mills Associates. A system of road signs directs visitors to the buildings, where colourful banners indicate that this is the gateway to the National and State Parks and to the downtown area.

Lowell, 30 miles north-west of Boston and the cradle of the American industrial revolution, was founded in 1826, but the first of its several great textile mills, the Lowell Mill, predates the city's foundation by four years. In its converted form it now provides the visitor centre to a rejuvenated city – for Lowell's golden age as America's first industrial city was short-lived. Decline set in as early as the second half of the nineteenth century with the establishment of new and more competitive manufacturing centres. Lowell was transformed from a Yankee mill town, with its workforce of mill girls, to a diverse working-class city employing cheaper immigrant labour. After the First World War, with the Southern textile factories taking the lead, Lowell's economy declined even further. By the 1970s the city was dying.

The turning point came in 1978 when Wang, a computer company with 12,000 new jobs to offer, was persuaded to relocate in Lowell. The newly formed Lowell Development and Financial Corporation (LDFC) was able to lend Wang the $5 million Urban Development Grant that the city council had obtained from federal sources. Like all others to the LDFC, the repayments, at 4 per cent over 25 years, go into a revolving fund, with 80 per cent assigned to industrial development, 10 per cent to neighbourhood improvements and 10 per cent to housing. Also in 1978, the Lowell National Historical Park was established by legislation, with the intention of turning Lowell into a 'living museum' and so attracting federal and state funding. The aim was to revitalize the local economy while at the same time communicating Lowell's historical message. It was to be a voluntary partnership involving federal, state and local interest as well as the private sector. In 1979 the Lowell Plan was established as a non-profit-making private development corporation, using private funds to support and stimulate development.

The legislation that created the Lowell National Historical Park also created the Lowell Historic Preservation Commission, an independent federal agency within the Department of the Interior, working closely with the Park. The Commission, with its 15 members representing local, state and federal interests, assists the National Park Service with management and preservation duties, and oversees the preservation district, which consists largely of privately owned properties. It exercises development authority and provides historic preservation grants and loans to private property owners, and cultural grants to a variety of individuals and organizations in the city. Projects it has helped finance and organize include the conversion of Lowell Mills, the revival of trams, the conversion of the Boott Mill Boarding House and the restoration of the Pawtucket Canal walkway.

Important for tourist development is the Lowell Heritage State Park, flagship of the Massachusetts urban state park system, which combines environmental improvements, historic preservation and educational exhibits. Having identified the state-owned canal system as the focus for future development, it has been responsible for the restoration of the canal locks and for the creation of the Eastern Canal Park. Here, a water-power exhibit illustrates the significance of the 30-feet (9-m) drop at Pawtucket Falls on the Merrimack River, which was the key to Lowell's rise to industrial prominence.

The Lowell Mills were re-opened as Market Mills in 1982, having been restored and converted into a visitor centre on the ground floor, and into 230 apartments, of which more than half are for the elderly, on the upper floors. From the car park a passageway carved out of the façade leads into the courtyard and to the visitor centre, which includes a reception desk,

Right: *Lowell Mills before conversion. Though damaged by fire and abandoned by their owners, who were unwilling even to pay property taxes, the mills were recognized by LHPC for their great re-use potential. Passing through a passageway carved out of the front building, the visitor now arrives in a lively public courtyard (below) where the landscaping provides an attractive setting for eating lunch, listening to music or meeting friends over a drink. The building on the left houses an art gallery and a number of artists and craftsmen, who can be seen at work. In the building on the right the visitor centre occupies part of the ground floor. The upper storeys of both buildings have been converted into apartments.*

The two-storey space of the visitor centre at Market Mills, where a slide show and an exhibition provide an introduction to the city and its history.

Boott Mills Boarding House before and after restoration (opposite). *The boarding house is one of only two surviving buildings which accommodated the mill girls. The substitution of flat roofs for pitched roofs and the blocking up of many windows had changed the building out of all recognition. In converting the building into a museum and library, what remained of the interior structure had to be gutted, and a completely new interior constructed within the old shell.*

exhibition area, museum store, and audio-visual and other education facilities. Across the courtyard artists and craftsmen, including weavers, can be seen at work and there is an art gallery which exhibits their products. There is also a food court with several ethnic fast food restaurants sharing a common eating area.

Boott Mill Boarding House, built around 1836 and one of only two surviving buildings that accommodated the Lowell mill girls, was re-opened in 1988 as the Patrick J. Mogan Cultural Center, named in honour of the educator and planner who developed the Lowell urban park concept. The exterior has been accurately restored, but the interiors are new, the original interiors having been lost in the course of earlier alterations and through neglect. What remained of the interior structure was completely removed before conversion, leaving the old building as an empty shell. A major new two-storey wing has been added to the back to accommodate the University Center for Lowell History. The restored building tells the story of the nation's industrial heritage through the lives of Lowell's working people. It includes a partially re-created boarding house interior, other historical and folk-life exhibits, archives, classrooms, offices and a library. A park for concerts and festivals is planned on adjoining land, and the Boott Mills themselves will open in 1990 as a museum of America's industrial revolution, with a gallery for temporary exhibitions and a theatre. Offices on the upper floors will serve as the headquarters for the Lowell National Historical Park as well as for the North Atlantic Cultural Resources Center of the National Park Service, which will consolidate regional personnel responsible for historic preservation, archaeology and museum curatorial care.

Leatherworks, London

Manufacturing premises into furniture showrooms

The exedra, or semi-circular textile room with shallow, glass-fronted cupboards recessed in the wall. The circular and octagonal shapes of the rooms have been created by forming a separate lining of panelled plasterboard fixed to metal framing within the existing walls of the building.

The group of three late nineteenth- and early twentieth-century buildings in a narrow street west of St Pancras Station were built by leather manufacturers and occupied by them until 1982. A politically doctrinaire local authority was unwilling to allow a change from industrial use, so the buildings remained vacant for four years while conversions to a ballet school, an accountancy college and artists' studios were in turn proposed but rejected. In 1986 a consortium of design companies bought the buildings and let the basement, ground and first floors of two of the buildings to Sunar, the new UK sister company of the US furniture manufacturers Sunar Hauserman. The local authority accepted the proposal for a showroom because Sunar were manufacturers.

The buildings were typically narrow and deep, and one of them had a shed at the back extending all the way to the next street, where there was a loading dock. This shed provided the large space required for the display of office furniture systems, and the loading dock was retained and modified. The ground floors of the two buildings were combined by making three openings in the party wall, and the space was subdivided into a sequence of small rooms of contrasting shape, fitted around the existing goods lift and staircases. The old entrance is re-used, but to avoid the goods lift the longitudinal axis is off-set on to the right-handed bay of the entrance hall, so that it runs past the semi-circular textile room into a drum, turns 45 degrees into an octagon and then straightens out again on to the axis of the entrance to penetrate the large office systems display area within the old shed. The three openings in the party wall provide a cross-axis centred on the semi-circular textile room.

Although the plan follows formal, classical principles, the surfaces that define the plan are about as impermanent as a stage set, though exquisitely crafted. The walls and ceilings, made of panelled plasterboard on metal framing, form a separate lining within the permanent structure of the building. The spaces between the walls resulting from alcoves, niches and octagonal forms, are used for service rooms, storage and ducts. The lighting is mainly artificial, except in the shed, where the existing roof lights have been adapted and operate in conjunction with artificial lighting.

Other parts of the buildings remained unusable until 1987 when a change in the planning laws made it possible to convert them into offices and studios. One building had a robust Victorian character, another was in the 'Egyptian' style. In the conversion the character of each part was respected, and the built-in furniture was detailed to reflect the different styles. Few changes were made to the exterior. Accretions such as awnings were removed, and common elements like windows and window frames imposed to unify the buildings and make them read as one.

The plan (above) *shows how the showroom spreads over the ground floors of two adjacent buildings. By re-using the old entrance it became impossible to create a sequence of spaces along a single axis, because the goods lift was in the way. The architect turned this difficulty to his advantage and has achieved a richer and far more interesting sequence. In the entrance hall* (right), *the reception desk opposite the main door blocks the way forward and forces the visitor to take a side-step, first to the right, and then to the left, before proceeding on his journey. 1 entrance hall; 2 reception area; 3 exedra for textiles; 4 showrooms; 5 boardroom; 6 furniture display; 7 lavatories; 8 kitchen; 9 store; 10 loading bay.*

In the octagonal room (left) chairs and fabrics are displayed in surrounding niches. This room returns the visitor to the primary axis of the street entrance and of the long showroom at the back, which is entered from it.

The robust Victorian street front (above) has remained largely unaltered, though a degree of unity has been imposed through common elements like windows and window frames.

The long shed at the back (opposite) has been transformed into a showroom for office furniture systems. The existing division into five bays has been retained. The room is spanned horizontally with large vaulted beams that are interrupted by the light from the clerestories. It is the only room that has natural light, though this is augmented with both incandescent and fluorescent lighting.

Tiefenbrunnen Mill, Zurich, Switzerland

Flour mill into multiple use

The group of buildings known as the Tiefenbrunnen Mill, or Wehrli Mühle after the family who owned and ran it for 70 years, stands in Zollikon, a lake-side suburb of Zurich a few miles south-east of the city. It was built in 1889 as a brewery, and consisted of two parallel buildings, with an administration block at one end and a stable block at the other. On one side the buildings were set against rising ground, which was held back with thick stone retaining walls. The main building on this side was the cooling house for cooling beer. On the higher ground above the stables was the paddock for the horses. In 1913 the main building was converted into a flour mill. These early two- and three-storey buildings had cast-iron columns, steel beams and jack-arches, and walls of yellow brick, with vertical and horizontal bands and arched decoration in red brick. In the 1930s a bulky reinforced concrete warehouse was built opposite the stables and the gap between the administration block and one end of the cooling house was filled with single-storey workshops. In 1983 operations were transferred to a factory outside Zurich and the mill was closed down.

The mill owner carried out the conversion himself by borrowing money. His intention from the beginning was to introduce a mix of uses to ensure that the place would remain alive day and night. That is why on the paddock there are now two parallel blocks containing 17 apartments. The central part of the main mill building has been lovingly restored and fitted up with a full complement of milling machinery to provide an extremely popular operational museum. The remainder of the mill building has shops and showrooms on the ground and basement floors, offices above and studios in the roof. The cooling house also has shops on the ground floor, so the space between the two buildings has become a street, at the end of which is a pit for outdoor shows and 'happenings'. A covered bridge connects the two buildings at first-floor level. The 1930s warehouse has had one bay removed to free the end of the mill building and to allow the construction of a lightly glazed, three-storey link between the two buildings. The warehouse has also been raised by a floor and re-clad externally with steel and glass, or panels of brick

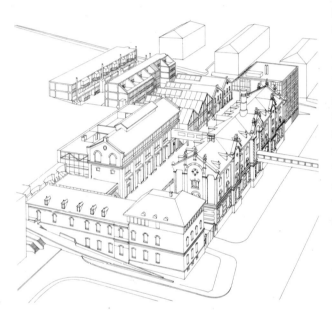

Bird's-eye view (above) *showing two parallel buildings (the main building and the cooling house), with an administration block at one end and a stable block at the other. Behind the stable block the old paddock has been developed with two parallel apartment blocks.*

The ground-floor plan (right) *shows how the buildings on one side — the single-storey workshop, cooling house and stables — are set against rising ground which is held back with thick stone retaining walls. The plan also shows the new workshop block between the stables and the cooling house, and the street between the parallel buildings, which ends in a pit for outdoor shows and 'happenings'.*

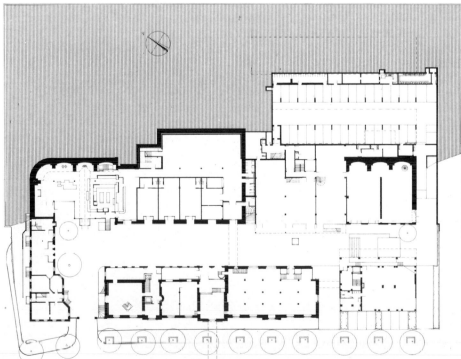

The central bay of the main mill building seen from the internal street, with the entrance into the mill museum, where a full complement of machinery demonstrates the complete milling process, including the baking of many varieties of bread. The chimney dates from the building's origin as a brewery.

The street between the parallel apartment blocks on the site of the former paddock. These new buildings make no attempt to imitate nineteenth-century industrial architecture and are constructed in reinforced concrete and prefabricated panels in aluminium frames.

The stable block has been converted into an art gallery, and the rough stone retaining wall at the back cleaned up and made into a feature. Removing the hayloft revealed the timber roof trusses and resulted in wonderful spaces. The rotted timber floorboards have been replaced with concrete.

A living room in one of the apartments housed in two new blocks on the former paddock. These not only help to finance the centre, but also keep it alive at night.

Above: *A furniture showroom in the basement of the main mill building. The old structure of heavy cast-iron columns and steel beams, encased in concrete for fire protection, can be clearly seen.*

Right: *The single-storey workshop which has been converted into a restaurant. Skylights have been introduced at the back to draw attention to the stone retaining wall.*

Between the administration block and the cooling house (top) an old workshop has been converted into a fashionable restaurant, while a small theatre has been created in the bowels of the old cooling house (above).

to suit its new function as open-plan computer offices with movable partitions.

With the exception of the front façade, the cooling house collapsed when it was unfrozen, and had to be rebuilt to its former profile with a new steel and concrete structure inside. The building now houses a 200-seat theatre in the basement, a dance hall, a television studio, workshops, and studios on the attic floor. A new workshop block has been built in steel and glass between the cooling house and the stables. The old workshops at the other end of the cooling house have been converted into a restaurant, and the stables with their lofty spaces into art galleries. In both buildings a feature has been made of the old stone retaining wall at the back.

As the City of Zurich had specified that the profile of the four older buildings should be retained, there was no question of adding any floors. It did not insist on faithful restoration or imitation, however, so it was possible to make use of thoroughly contemporary materials – reinforced concrete and aluminium – and to add new elements, both inside and out. These are clearly of the late twentieth century, as, for example, the glazed roof over the single-storey extension to the mill building and the continuous glazing of the attic storey in the cooling house.

The new connecting bridge of steel and glass between the 1930s warehouse and the main mill building. One bay of the warehouse was demolished to free the end wall of the mill building, which had to be rebuilt. The warehouse itself was raised by a floor and completely re-clad in steel and glass.

Lemsford Mill, Welwyn Garden City, UK

Water mill into workshops and house

Lemsford Mill, a small brick and timber-clad water mill on the outskirts of Welwyn Garden City, Hertfordshire, was originally a flour mill that generated its power from an undershot water-wheel straddling the River Lea. Mentioned in the Domesday Book, it is known to have been a two-storey structure in 1760 and was rebuilt in 1863. The river flowing beneath the building drops nearly 6 feet (1.75 m) at the mill race. Michael and Pauline Ayling bought the listed mill, which had fallen into disrepair, the adjacent millhouse, outbuildings and 2½ acres (1 hectare) of surrounding garden and river bank. The intention was for the mill to be used for the small family business, which manufactures electro-magnetic control equipment, and for the Aylings to move into the millhouse.

Before undertaking the mill conversion proper, it was necessary to stabilize the undercroft of the mill. The design of the conversion respects the solidity of the existing brick and timber building, brings its existing fabric into good repair and upgrades its thermal performance. Its character is reinforced by the addition of new elements, mainly of welded tubular steel and galvanized steel gratings, whose lightweight appearance sets up a visual counterpoint of old and new. This attitude is applied to all new external elements – the new road-bridge, footbridges, entrance deck and external structures – and also passes into the building in the form of stairs, handrails, screens and furniture in a continuing sequence.

The visitor, on approaching the mill, is made to experience the presence of the river by passing over and along it. The mill itself is entered at first-floor level, parallel to the direction of the river flow, which then remains visible through a vertical glazed slot extending the full height of the building. Vertical movement within the mill is through an open well that increases in size and thus develops a feeling of space and the sense of being able to look through and from the building. Elements placed within the mill are separated from the external walls to enhance the feeling of the original 'shell' as a single space,

In converting Lemsford Mill for a manufacturing company the architect has purposely confronted old and heavy building elements, like brick walls, cast-iron columns and timber trusses, with light and elegant tubular steelwork. Below, left: *The new staircase inside the converted mill, wrapped around and supported on a central newel post, and* (below, right) *the road bridge on the north side of the mill. The entrance to the mill is on the south side via a footbridge and drawbridge, which make use of the same tubular steel details.*

while the external–internal relationship is reinforced, and additional daylight gained by the single, extended glazed slot, which avoids either destroying or copying the patterns of the existing windows.

Within the mill three basic but separate functions occur: office space on the top floor, workshops on the second floor, entry and storage at first-floor level, and further storage and plant-room space on the lower ground floor. It was vital to avoid sound transference from the workshop to the other spaces and yet to exploit the volume of the existing building as a three-dimensional experience. A considerable amount of landscaping has been carried out, and part of the rear of the millhouse has been removed and replaced by a fully glazed, two-storey addition, which exploits new spatial relationships between the house, the river and the existing garden.

The top floor under the timber roof trusses, with the top of the new staircase and the balustrade of tubular steel continuing around the well, which has been cut to make visual connections between the floors. The central newel post, also of tubular steel, is fixed at the top to one of the roof trusses.

New Mills, Wotton-under-Edge, UK

Water mill into high-tech offices

New Mills (above) is a multi-storey brick building with cast-iron windows and a slate roof. It retains its water system intact, but its most distinctive feature is probably the slim clock tower with its Dutch gable.

New Mills, with its pond, culverts and outfall, is a landmark in its Cotswold setting, and this is officially recognized by its Grade-II* listing. A large multi-storey building of 1790, the mill originally relied on water power and today retains its water system intact. In 1980 it was acquired by Renishaw Metrology, a company concerned with probes and probe systems essential to the new machine tools, who were attracted primarily by the production space offered by other buildings on the site. It was only after an unsuccessful competition for a new office block elsewhere on the site that it was decided in 1983 to convert the old mill, the company accepting the argument that an old building would be more memorable to its mainly German, Japanese and American clients than a brand new one.

The building has robust brick walls with cast-iron windows and a slate roof, and an internal structure of cast-iron columns supporting heavy timber beams. It had deteriorated badly after its last users, weavers of narrow elasticated fabric, had abandoned it, and a considerable amount of repair work was necessary to bring the mill back into a usable state. None of this, except for the rebuilding of a gable wall, has left its mark on the exterior, the

The ground-floor plan (right) shows how the accommodation required by a high technology industry has been fitted freely within the rectilinear brick shell and around the cast-iron and timber structure of the old building. The new staircases (opposite) are placed clear of the original wall but allow people using them a view out of the window. Keeping them clear of the wall also allows room for curved landings, which give the tubular steel balustrade full play.

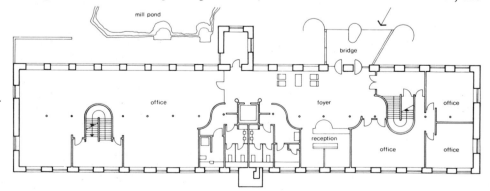

Looking down into the entrance foyer from the first-floor gallery. The existing floor structure was cut back to the column line to form the two-storey space. The balustrade is mainly of tubular steel, but the handrail, partitions and gallery edge are in beech, their curvilinear forms standing out in contrast to the angular character of the existing building.

greatest bonus perhaps being the retention of the cast-iron windows, which had survived in reasonable condition.

Inside the building, on the other hand, considerable changes have taken place, though the original structure remains everywhere visible. Two new steel staircases and a lift shaft have been inserted, and an entrance foyer two storeys high has been created by partly cutting away the floor structure to form a balcony. Some of the new elements, such as the entrance bridge, the balustrade in the double-height foyer, and the structure of the new stairs, are in steel, but it is the new beech joinery and its mainly curvilinear forms that stand out as a contrast to the angular and four-square character of the existing building. The benefits of this are two-fold: the new is clearly distinguished from the old, and the difficulty of aligning necessarily precise new work with the existing irregular fabric is avoided. It demonstrates yet again how additions to historic buildings should express their own time, creating striking contrasts or harmonious fusion between old elements and new, rather than attempting simply to re-create the forms of the past.

A detail of the east front with the clock tower. The original cast-iron windows and tie plates have all been preserved.

Lone Star Brewery, San Antonio, USA

Brewery into museum of fine art

The conversion of the Lone Star Brewery in San Antonio, Texas, into the San Antonio Museum of Art shows once again the versatility of nineteenth-century industrial buildings. The new interiors are wholly convincing and it is hard to imagine them used for any other purpose, least of all brewing.

The brewery occupies a five-acre site on the banks of the San Antonio River, and consists of a large brewhouse with twin castellated towers and seven ancillary structures. Built between 1895 and 1904 to the designs of E. Jungerfeld and Co. of St Louis (assisted by Wahrenberger and Beckman of San Antonio), it prospered until Prohibition led to a change of use as the Lone Star Cotton Mills (1921–25). When this operation also failed, the buildings were divided into individual units and occupied by small businesses until 1971, when the San Antonio Museum Association bought the whole site. In 1972 the brewery was entered in the USA's National Register of Historic Places, and in 1973 architects were appointed and a feasibility study was begun.

So far only the brewhouse and storehouse have been converted, leaving plenty of scope for expansion. The construction is of cast-iron columns and steel beams, supporting a floor structure of brick and concrete vaults that has

The impressive street elevation of the old brewery (above) has had several windows bricked up to protect the interior from excess daylight, and its suspended bridge has been replaced by a steel and tinted glass footbridge. The lower central part houses the entrance lobby (opposite).

The lifts of the San Antonio Museum of Art (right) are transparent showcases for the moving cabs and their mechanism. Shaft and cab are mainly of glass, with walls of mirror and working parts of chromium plate. The top and bottom of the cab are covered with tiny lights, and the effect is magical.

The Mexican folk art displayed in the museum is seen to best advantage in a bright top-floor gallery in the west tower. The Plexiglass and aluminium showcase is a design developed specially for this installation.

Nineteenth-century brickwork is reflected in the tinted glass of the twentieth-century footbridge linking the east and west towers, softening the transition between old and new.

an excellent load-bearing capacity. The external walls are yellow brick with numerous large arched window openings in the Romanesque style, which was fashionable at the time. Many of these windows have been bricked up to protect the exhibits from too much light. Other windows have been given single large panes of tinted glass instead of having their many panes and elaborate mullions and transoms restored.

In the brewhouse each floor of both towers was already divided into two spacious rooms suitable for galleries. The design solution was to devise a circulation that enabled people to take a lift up the west tower, stopping on each floor to visit the galleries; then cross to the east tower by the steel and tinted glass footbridge that replaces the old suspended bridge, pausing on the roof terrace or in the cafeteria; and walk down the open stair of the east tower. The two towers are connected by a lower central section which provides an

After crossing from the west, or higher tower to the east tower by means of the footbridge, the visitor descends one flight to the roof terrace and café, before continuing downwards and back to the ground-floor galleries, entrance lobby and gift shop.

ideal entrance hall with auditorium and gift shop. The hall, which is double-height and top-lit, has a staircase leading to a gallery which gives access to the upper part of the raked auditorium floor.

Future proposals include the conversion of the storage building immediately behind the brewhouse into conservation and administrative offices, shops and library functions; the conversion of the hops house into a restaurant; the creation of a sculpture garden at the east end of the site; and the development of the river banks with walkways, facilities for boat traffic, landscaping and lighting, as a continuation of the Paseo del Rio in downtown San Antonio.

155

Municipal Asphalt Plant, New York

Industrial plant into sports hall and cultural centre

The small double-height gym at first-floor level. The gallery around the gym at second-floor level provides access to the art and photography studios.

One of New York's great monuments of twentieth-century industrial architecture, the Municipal Asphalt Plant on East River Drive at 91st Street, has been converted into a sports and arts centre with an artificially turfed playing field on the adjacent open site. Designed in 1944 by the engineers Kahn and Jacobs, it has a parabolic form that was a response to the asphalt-making process, which consisted of mixing the asphalt on the upper level of the plant and dropping it into trucks waiting below. The structure consists of four prefabricated lightweight steel trusses with concrete panels between, so that the building is 90 feet (27 m) high but only 66 feet (20 m) from front to back.

When the plant ceased operating in 1968, the intention was to demolish it and develop the whole five-acre (two-hectare) site with housing and a school. In 1972 George Murphy, professor of pathology at New York Hospital – Cornell Medical Center and a local resident, joined in the fight to save the building, arguing that in a neighbourhood already twice as dense as Manhattan as a whole, community facilities and open recreational space for youth were needed, rather than housing. In 1976 the plant was declared a New York City Landmark and in 1980 it was listed on the National Register of Historic Places. The Neigborhood Committee, with Dr Murphy as chairman, finally persuaded the city to sponsor the centre with a special grant, providing the committee operated and maintained the building at its own

The abandoned asphalt plant (above) has a distinctive parabolic form – a response to the asphalt-making process, which consisted of mixing the asphalt on the upper level of the plant and then dropping it into trucks waiting below. In converting the plant, the engineers Kahn and Jacobs used four lightweight steel ribs, prefabricated in three sections to simplify reinforcement. Ninety feet high and twenty-two feet apart, they support a series of barrel vaults made up of concrete panels.

The large gymnasium (right) occupies more than half the height of the plant at the top of the building, where the asphalt used to be mixed. The 'wasted' space below the peak, which formerly contained an exhaust fan, is now put to good use as a jogging track. Seating can be rolled out to accommodate 140 spectators.

expense. The conversion, which was completed in October 1985, consisted of subdividing the building into a four-storey structure, with the first three floors relatively low and containing the entrance hall, offices, theatre, small gym, art studio, darkroom and classrooms. This leaves more than half the height for the top floor, where a large gym with a high-level running track occupies the whole space. The entrance hall, which runs from front to back, and in parts rises through the three lower storeys, occupies the space of the former driveway that passed through the building.

The underground tunnels, which used to carry asphalt, now store chilled water as part of an energy-conservation programme, most of the equipment being housed separately behind the building.

In its reincarnation the Asphalt Plant is proving immensely successful, with private schools renting the gym, and pupils from parochial and public schools taking art, photography and graphic design courses during the day; older children use the centre in the late afternoon, and adults in the evening. Musical and theatrical events are held regularly in the 93-seat theatre on the ground floor.

Chewing Gum and Battery factories, New York

Factories into design centre

Design centres, of which there are a number in the United States, have been compared with multi-level suburban shopping malls, where customers move from store to store in search of their favourite merchandise. In a design centre architects, interior designers and the trade move from showroom to showroom in search of the most comfortable chair or the most efficient office furniture. The New York International Design Center is located in Long Island City, a section of the Borough of Queens, which faces Manhattan across the East River; it consists of four adjacent buildings dating from the First World War and constructed of cast-in-place concrete. Together these buildings will provide two million square feet (186,000 m^2) of space, but for the time being only two have been converted – the American Chicle Company chewing gum factory (Center I), and the Eveready Battery factory (Center II). Center III, the former Sunshine Biscuit factory, and Center IV, its companion garage, together accounting for half the floor area, will also be converted providing the owner and developer, Lazard Realty, can persuade New York's contract and residential furnishings industry to leave Manhattan – where it is fragmented all over the city – for a centralized location, in what is still seen by many as an industrial wasteland.

The original entrances in Thomson Avenue on the north side of the factories have been retained, but new main entrances have been created at a lower level on the south and west sides. These open onto a plaza, which is now a parking lot but which will eventually become a landscaped square with two levels of parking underneath. The south façade of the Center II building, the first to be converted, was never finished with the brick and terracotta veneer that the three street façades received. The two wings were left so that they could be expanded southwards, with the gap between admitting freight wagons into the open court. Visitors enter through the gap, past the new lift tower and into the court, where the rail tracks have been replaced with a terrazzo floor. The eight levels of galleries that surround the court provide a nine-feet-wide (2.7 m) promenade, and beyond lie the showrooms, which are separated from the promenade by a glass wall. Having made the tour of its showrooms, visitors can cross over upper-level bridges into Center I to the east, and when Center III is completed they will be able to do the same to the west.

The plan (right) *shows the three factories and garage which will eventually make up the New York International Design Center. So far, only the two right-hand factories have been converted into Center I and Center II.*

Center I (opposite) *occupies the whole rectangular site and is by far the longest building. The view of the interior, which shows less than half its length, is from the central lift tower which divides the court in two. The court was originally open to the sky, but has been covered with translucent plastic skylights to transform it into a covered atrium. Both halves are surrounded by five levels of galleries connected by cascading stairs. The concrete walls, columns and ceilings have been repaired and painted.*

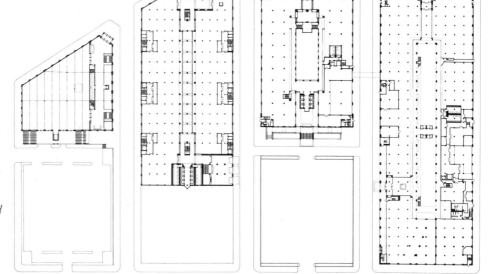

The court of Center II has also been covered with translucent plastic skylights and is surrounded by eight levels of galleries. The view to the north (above) shows a symmetrical arrangement of new staircases meeting on a central landing, which is original, while the view to the south (above, right) shows the new lift tower and entrance from the plaza. The oblong openings to the surrounding galleries were originally windows, which have been removed. The steel catwalks at third-floor level lower the ceiling plane for people on the ground floor and also provide the means of suspending lighting, sound equipment and decorative banners.

Center I, completed in 1986 shortly after Center II, also has a sky-lit central atrium surrounded by showrooms, but because it is a lower and much longer building, the lift tower was placed at the centre of the atrium and new steel staircases were run in cascading form down each half. An new arcade incorporating the main entrance has been recessed into the west façade corresponding to the length of the plaza.

Except for the south façade of Center II, which was resurfaced in stucco, the existing materials have been restored as far as possible to retain the industrial character of the buildings. The brick and terracotta veneer of Center II has been extensively repaired and painted, as have the concrete walls, columns and ceilings of Center I. The original tilework on the exterior walls of Center I has also been cleaned, and missing units have been replaced.

The creation of the Center is a prime example of how space provided by a group of rather ordinary industrial buildings can be used for a commercial purpose. It is for economic and social, rather than historical reasons, that the range of potentially useful redundant buildings is today virtually unlimited.

Part of the long side elevation of Center I (above) with the bridge connecting Center I with Center II on the left. The south side of Center II (right) has become the main entrance elevation, where previously it had been the unfinished back of the factory, with a gap between the two wings for freight wagons to pass into the open court. In the conversion the two wings have been tied together at the top by a deep beam, and at the bottom by a barrel-vaulted canopy to make a gateway out of the gap.

Templeton Factory, Glasgow, UK

Carpet factory into business centre

The Templeton Factory on Glasgow Green has been converted into a business centre, containing 145 units expressly for start-up businesses and the relocation of small firms in the area. Although James Stewart-Templeton began manufacturing carpets on the site in 1856, the first buildings to survive – Building 3 and the magnificent 'Doge's Palace' (Building 5) by the Scottish architect William Leiper – were not built until 1897 and 1898 respectively, by which time new buildings were required to meet the demands of an expanding trade and to house the recently developed machinery for weaving Axminster carpets. By 1963 the company had developed the whole site with a ring of five- and six-storey buildings surrounding a courtyard of single-storey weaving sheds. Changes in world trade and manufacturing techniques, however, led to the buildings' becoming uneconomic to operate, and the company moved to a modern factory in 1978, leaving the Glasgow factory empty and threatened with total demolition. Fortunately, the Glasgow Eastern Area Renewal (GEAR) project, a major inner-city initiative created and coordinated by the Scottish Development Agency (SDA) to regenerate one of the larger areas of urban dereliction in the UK, decided otherwise and undertook the conversion of the factory in four phases, starting in 1980 and finishing in 1986.

A feasibility study revealed that the structure, general condition and load-bearing capacity of the perimeter buildings were good, while the central courtyard and buildings were semi-derelict. Work began, therefore, with the central courtyard being cleared and Buildings 1 and 4 being converted into offices (Building 1) and workshops (Building 4). The ground floor of Building 1, which was found to be in particularly good condition, having been Templeton's office suite, has been occupied by the Business Development Bureau, another SDA initiative to provide advice and practical help for small enterprises.

The second phase concentrated on Buildings 2 and 3. The ground floors of Building 2, dating from 1934, have been converted into light industrial premises, and the upper floors into office and studio accommodation. In this building the Charles Robertson Partnership, architects for the business centre, have converted two standard office units into offices for themselves, making effective use of an existing timber and steel-hung mezzanine floor

The 'Doge's Palace', built in 1898 to the designs of William Leiper. The original proposal for a museum having been rejected, the building has been converted into a 'mid-technology centre'. It is hoped that it will attract a mix of uses, reflecting a breakdown of the traditionally accepted divisions between office, laboratory and production space.

previously used for yarn storage. Building 3, dating from 1897, has been converted into workshops and into accommodation for further education projects with special emphasis on micro-technology.

The third phase concentrated on Building 6, dating from 1934, which has been converted into a mixture of light industrial and workshop/office space. And the final phase transformed the 'Doge's Palace' (Building 5) into a 'mid-technology centre' to provide accommodation for the rapidly advancing technologies of electronics and telecommunications, bio-technology and opto-electronics.

The centre now houses over a hundred small businesses spanning both the manufacturing and service sectors. Service areas, access, toilets, security, building insurance and other ancillary services are maintained centrally by the SDA and covered by a service charge. Conference and meeting rooms are provided to serve the needs of the whole GEAR area. The fact that the centre is open 24 hours a day, with security covering all common areas, brings the area to life.

Ligure Latta factory, Genoa, Italy

Tinplate factory into community centre

The Centro Civico Communale in Sanpierdarena, a dense and deprived suburb of Genoa, is just one of many impressive community centres built by the Italians. Completed in 1986, it makes use of a factory, long since abandoned, built by the Liguria Tinplate Company in the early years of the twentieth century. There was nothing special about the building except that it was already in existence, it was soundly built of reinforced concrete and, with its three storeys and two unequal parallel blocks linked in the middle, it provided the required space. Today the building houses three multi-purpose halls, an auditorium, a library, a gymnasium, a secondary school, an art gallery, a canteen, various service rooms and administrative offices.

At ground level the external wall of the old factory has been broken into, and covered arcades have been created with recessed entrances under the building. The pedestrian 'street' between the parallel blocks is now continuous, with entrances to right and left passing under the double-height gymnasium block, which stretches across the full width of the site. The activities housed on the ground floor – those with the highest amount of public participation – are the multi-purpose halls of the community centre proper, the canteen and the art gallery, the circular or octagonal forms of which are set back within the arcades, but clearly visible from outside. The school is a separate three-storey block at the northern end of the site, but here too the external wall at ground level has been set back to form a recess for the entrance and caretaker's flat.

At first-floor level, over the community centre and art gallery respectively, are the children's and the adults' library, linked by a bridge over the 'street'. At second-floor level, over the children's library, is the 250-seat auditorium designed for debates, film shows and theatrical performances; and over the adults' library are the changing rooms for the gymnasium which has a public gallery with 285 seats. Over the auditorium and gymnasium the large spans required a new steel roof structure, while the existing flat roofs over the school and changing rooms were easily adaptable as roof gardens, though inadequate safety requirements have since brought about their closure and inevitable deterioration.

The drawing shows, on the top line, the north elevation, with the school on the right and the pedestrian 'street' passing under the gymnasium in the middle; and the south elevation overlooking the railway viaduct, with the auditorium on the left and the library on the right. The middle and bottom lines show the elevations overlooking the pedestrian 'street' and, in section, the central connecting block of the gymnasium.

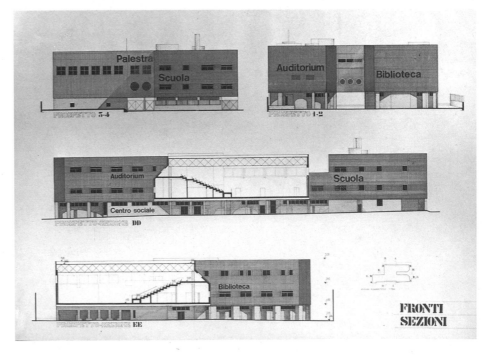

The auditorium block and the pedestrian 'street' between the parallel blocks seen from the railway viaduct. The view shows the centre in its setting of a dense and deprived suburb. The old factory has been 'wrapped' in a corrugated aluminium cladding, painted blue and yellow.

The structure and recessed walls of the ground floor have been plastered and painted grey, while the upper floors have been 'wrapped' in a corrugated aluminium cladding, painted blue to denote education and culture, and yellow to denote sport. The building in its new guise recalls the simple packaging of consumer goods or the containers which can be seen stacked up in the nearby port. The effect, reinforced by giant graphics, is to announce the presence of this social and cultural centre to all around, and to bring more than a touch of brightness to a drab area of the city.

165

The auditorium (left) and the gymnasium (above) are the largest spaces in the centre. The former, with a seating capacity of 300, has been designed for debates, film and slide shows, and theatrical or musical performances. The latter is officially approved for volley-ball matches, but can also be used for basket-ball, hand-ball and gymnastics.

The school is on the Via d'Aste (opposite) with the entrance under the building from the pedestrian 'street'. The external wall of the old factory has generally been broken into at ground level to form covered arcades with recessed entrances.

5 Ecclesiastical Buildings

Meeting house

Temple

Church

Priory

Monastery

St Oswald's Old Church at Fulford, near York, has been converted into a private house. The nave and chancel now serve as dining hall and parlour, but remain virtually unchanged. They also serve as exhibition space for the owner's collection of medieval works of art and furniture.

The decline of religious observance and the growth of suburbia have caused churches all over the world to lose their congregations and become redundant. In most European countries churches that are listed as historic monuments are maintained and repaired with public funds. Redundancy and the need to find a new use become the responsibility of central or local government. The restoration and conversion into museums after the Second World War of some of the Romanesque churches in Cologne, for example, was financed by the city and *Land* jointly. In Basle the fourteenth-century Franciscan convent church underwent a major restoration and was converted into a history museum, all at the expense of the city. In England, however, Ecclesiastical Exemption, which gives the Church of England complete independence but at the same time denies it any state aid in looking after the fabric of its many buildings, has resulted in an elaborate process that is not always in the best interests of the building concerned. The Pastoral Measure of 1968 allows a church to be declared redundant, ownership passing from the incumbent temporarily to the diocese. A special committee of the diocese is then given a maximum of one year to find a new use for the church and to sell the church to the successful applicant, who carries out the conversion. Unfortunately, the maximum time is often exceeded, and the church falls prey to vandalism and theft, leaving it with the lead stripped off its roof and the rain pouring in, windows smashed, and ornamental features either broken or stolen.

At the same time churches are usually landmarks in their surroundings and traditionally a focal point of their community, so that their disappearance constitutes a serious loss. For this reason it is vital that sympathetic new uses are found that will damage neither the exterior nor the character of the church. An appropriate new use is one that fits both the spirit and the form of a church. This means public or community use, with a degree of ritual and ceremonial attached. It also means a use that maintains the single volume of the church or, at least, in the case of medieval or Victorian Gothic churches, the single volume of the nave. Uses that require the subdivision of the interior with floors and partitions are undesirable.

This means that churches do not generally make good houses, and least of all, apartment blocks. St Oswald's Old Church at Fulford in Yorkshire (p.180) is a special case where conversion into a private house was achieved without subdividing the nave and chancel. Its owner, moreover, has instigated projects and social events that have opened the 'house' to visitors and to a wide circle of friends, so maintaining the church's community function. The Charles Street Meeting House in Boston, also illustrated in this chapter (p.174), is another special case, where the subdivision of the space into offices and an apartment has not only been carried out with exceptional skill, but is wholly reversible, in case anyone in the future should want to turn the building back into a church. In most cases, however, where the single space of a church has been subdivided into an aggregation of small rooms, there ceases to be any correspondence between the exterior form and the interior volume, and all that can be said in favour of such projects is that the church has been saved as a familiar landmark in the town.

There is little ritual or ceremonial that goes with domestic use. Concerts and theatre, on the other hand, not only require the use of the undivided volume but are both public and ceremonial functions. The best type for conversion to a concert hall or theatre is the classical church, which is not divided into nave and two aisles, and is often even without columns. St James

St George's Brandon Hill at Bristol is a neo-classical church dating from the second decade of the nineteenth century. It is being converted into a concert hall by the Bristol architects Ferguson Mann. Within, a new timber stage has been inserted; the pews and gallery seating have been retained, and the marble lectern, pulpit and altar rail dismantled and stored for possible re-use under the stage.

the Less in Guernsey (p.182) is a fine example. With their box-like shape classical churches also tend to have good acoustics; and they often contain galleries, which provide extra seating with good visibility, and spacious crypts, which extend under the whole church, offering space for green rooms, cafeterias, dressing rooms and storage. A well-known and successful conversion to concert use dating from 1968, is St John's Smith Square, in London, which is a baroque church of 1730 by Thomas Archer. Ten years later a fine neo-classical church at Newington, Edinburgh, was converted into the Queen's Hall for the Scottish Philharmonic Society, and at about the same time, in 1976, St George's Brandon Hill at Bristol – a church built to the designs of Sir Robert Smirke, architect of the British Museum – was being tested for its suitability for the performance of chamber music. In 1977 the St George's Music Trust was formed with the purpose of converting the church, which was found to have a perfect acoustic for music, into a small concert hall. St George's is unusual in having its portico and steeple at the east end, where a stage has replaced the high altar and where the circular space under the dome of the steeple is now occupied by the green room. So far only the church has been converted, with the consequent lack of facilities like changing rooms, restaurant and instrument store. All these facilities will be provided in the crypt when sufficient money has been raised by the Trust.

The conversion of a church into a theatre is less common, but there are nevertheless some remarkable examples. In Bologna the baroque Jesuit church, Santa Lucia, is being converted into a centre for the performing arts, for the use of the university, the municipality and the city theatre. St George's in Tufnell Park, a north London red-brick suburb, was built in 1867 to the designs of George Truefitt and consists of a circular nave, a chancel with semi-circular apse, and a free-standing tower, which dominates the surrounding residential area. Reputedly based on a Crusader church in Salonika, the plan of the church was ideal for an Elizabethan-style theatre. The church ceased to be used for worship in 1963, but was not sold by the diocese until 1973. The first production of a Shakespeare play was staged in 1976, and the former church has been used regularly for performances of Elizabethan plays ever since. In Houston, Texas, there is an interesting example of a synagogue which was converted into a theatre at about the same time as St George's and also opened in 1976. The brown brick building with a monumental cast concrete portico was erected in 1924 to the designs of Joseph Finger. When in 1965 the congregation moved to a new suburban synagogue, the building was bought by the Houston Independent School District, which used it at first to house various adult education programmes. In 1971 the High School for the Performing and Visual Arts was founded and established itself there, while embarking at the same time on an extensive programme of remodelling and extending the existing building.

Other examples of churches successfully adapted to cultural uses include the Church of the Raising of the Holy Cross in Prague, converted into an arts centre, and the Hospitalet church in Ibiza (p.184), which can be both an art gallery and a concert room. The last example differs from the normal conversion in that it retains its church function as well as accommodating other compatible uses.

Conversion to museum use, which also falls into the cultural category, probably requires the least change to a church, and from that point of view is a highly desirable option, as it would be a relatively simple matter to reverse the process and convert the museum back into a church. The fact that the

The former High Victorian Unitarian chapel at Nottingham, converted into a museum of lace and now called the Lace Hall. The architect of the conversion, and now one of the directors of the museum, is Andrew James.

All Saints at Oxford, successfully converted into a college library by Robert Potter of the Brandt, Potter and Hare Partnership.

building remains public and that visiting a museum is generally a quiet and contemplative activity also make it an appropriate use. Gothic churches are especially well suited, as their division into nave and aisles, far from being restricting, as it is in the case of theatre or concert use, becomes a positive advantage in that it produces the variety of space needed for museum display. A great many churches have been converted into museums. One of the most spectacular examples is the Franciscan church in Basle, which has become a museum of church art. The English county town of Colchester has no less than two: Holy Trinity, converted into a museum of agricultural implements, and All Saints, converted into a museum of natural history. In Nottingham the former Unitarian chapel of 1874, which contains a fine collection of Victorian and Edwardian stained glass, has been converted into a museum of lace, while in Washington the former Masonic Temple Lodge of 1908 is now the Museum of Women in the Arts.

Other appropriate uses fall, broadly speaking, into two categories: educational and social. Heritage centres, which inform the local community about its architectural history and provide a forum for discussing new developments, can be regarded as offering a combination of museum and educational facilities. St Michael's at Chester, UK, has successfully served this purpose ever since it became redundant some fifteen years ago.

Churches make excellent libraries, providing a feeling of the single volume of the original structure is retained. One of the finest examples is All Saints at Oxford, a classical church built in 1699 and converted into a library for Lincoln College in 1975. The medieval church of St Peter in the East, also at Oxford, preceded All Saints by some five years in being converted into a library for St Edmund Hall. The nave was used for the reading area, the north chapel accommodated the law library, and the tower was formed into a six-storey stack for the storage of books not in current use. At Juterborg in the German Democratic Republic the late medieval Mönchenkirche is now a library and theatre, while in Houston the Central Church of Christ, built as recently as 1946, was considered worth converting into a public library. Here, the single volume of the interior has been subdivided with an upper floor, but this has been kept clear of the outer walls so that some feeling of the original space survives. Included in this chapter is a Theosophical temple (p. 178), also dating from the twentieth century, where the single volume of the interior has remained unaltered.

In the social category are churches converted into community centres, parish centres, youth centres and old people's day centres. All are worthy and not inappropriate uses, though they are more liable to require subdivision of the interior space then a concert hall, a museum or a library. Inappropriate uses, because they require the subdivision of the church or because the activity is not in the right spirit, are office, retail, restaurant and night-club use, of which there are regrettably too many examples around the world.

Monasteries, priories and convents are a different matter, even if their churches present the same problems as all other churches. Monasteries are generally made up of a large number of buildings which consist of a multitude of rooms of different size, thus offering great flexibility of use. The two examples in this chapter, Petershausen priory at Constance (p. 188) and the Ittingen Carthusian monastery in Switzerland (p. 190) demonstrate the great variety of uses possible: office, school, music academy, archive centre, museum, conference centre, social centre, hostel, restaurant, banqueting hall and workshop. Like Ittingen, the monastery of Santa Maria la Real at Aguilar

The chapel of the Ursuline convent at San Antonio, Texas, which is now used for assembly and general cultural activities, the convent as a whole having been converted into a craft centre. The architects of the conversion were Ford, Powell and Carson.

de Campo in Spain has been converted into an education centre. At Mons in Belgium a seventeenth-century convent is now the Royal Music Conservatoire, and at Parma in Italy there are plans to convert the Charterhouse into a museum of fashion. At Fall River in Massachusetts a convent consisting of several buildings has been converted into old people's and family housing. A more modest example is the late medieval nunnery of Agnietenhof at Zutphen in the Netherlands, where many of the buildings were being used for storage and industrial purposes and were rapidly falling into a state of dereliction. In the early 1970s the Wijnhuisfonds Foundation acquired the buildings and began selling them individually on condition that the buyer restore and convert them to an appropriate use. Most of the buildings are now private houses, and the central court has been paved and landscaped for communal use. In the case of the charming mid-nineteenth-century Ursuline convent at San Antonio in Texas, an educational use has been found. It has become the Southwest Craft Center and now houses a craft school, an exhibition gallery and a restaurant, with the beautiful chapel providing space for assembly and general cultural activities.

It is evident that the monastery, priory or convent, with its great variety of buildings of mainly cellular nature, is more readily adaptable to new uses than the church, even if the sheer scale of the operation is often daunting. The church presents a very particular challenge to the architect or developer, both because of its structural peculiarities and because of public sensitivity to its conversion. Treated with thoughtful respect, however, church conversions can be rewarding, offering unique qualities of mood and materials, form and location.

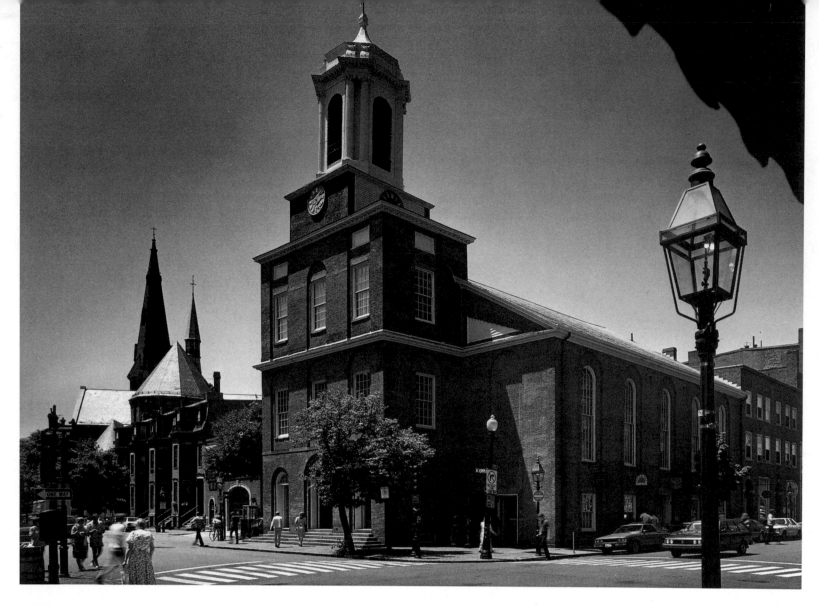

Charles Street Meeting House, Boston, USA

Meeting house into architect's studio, office and apartment

The Charles Street Meeting House stands on the corner of Charles Street and Mount Vernon in Boston. The main entrance is in the tower, as it has always been. The basement and upper parts of the tower contain an apartment with four bedrooms and three reception rooms. On the ground floor the body of the church accommodates shops, and the two upper floors, two suites of offices. Except for modest shop signs, the external appearance of the building remains unaltered.

Right: The reception area of the architect's office, with one of the original church clocks suspended, together with its exposed mechanism, from the vaulted ceiling above. The bell comes from the tower of the church. Clock and bell adjoin the conference room and have been set up to keep time and toll the hours, albeit quietly.

At the foot of Mount Vernon in Boston, Massachusetts, stands the Charles Street Meeting House, designed in 1807 by Asher Benjamin for the Third Baptist Church. Today it is listed in the USA's National Register of Historic Places and has been converted into an architect's home, his office and another office let by him, with shops on the ground floor.

The site of the Meeting House was originally by the side of the Charles River, high tide in those days coming up to the bottom of Beacon Hill. Since then several congregations have owned the building, the last, the Unitarian-Universalist Association, dissolving in 1978. In its last years before conversion the Meeting House was used only sporadically and fell into serious disrepair. In 1980 it was bought by the Charles Street Meeting House Associates with the intention of restoring the exterior and finding viable and compatible new uses for the interior. The conversion was completed in summer 1982, but only after the new owner had obtained a change in the deed restriction, which had required that the building be used only for religious, educational or cultural purposes.

The architect has preserved the outside of the building and has kept what has survived of the interior fabric intact, the interior furnishings having been lost in a fire. Columns, capitals, arches and ceiling decoration remain, and it would be possible to remove everything that has been added and restore the interior to its original condition. Five shops occupy most of the ground floor,

174

The living room of the apartment on the third floor of the tower is entered through a circular opening. The spiral stair leads to the library above, which is in the space formerly occupied by the church bell. From the library it is possible to go higher still by ship's ladder, up to the look-out in the lantern.

with individual entries from a lobby on Charles Street. Signs projecting from the building have been allowed for these shops. The three doors of the main entrance have been placed on sliding tracks to fit into side pockets during office hours. They are pulled closed at night so that the exterior looks unchanged. New double-glazed windows have been fitted inside the existing small-pane sash windows to preserve the existing fenestration.

The office space occupies most of the first, second and third floors, the architect's office with its double-height space and gallery recalling the space of the original church and being particularly successful. The residence, which

The architect's office on the second floor occupies four of the church's bays and a little more than half the width. The new floor is an extension of the old balconies. The arches and column capitals were repaired, and a mezzanine was installed, which is accessible by an elegant spiral staircase.

has a separate entrance off an existing private courtyard at the corner of Mount Vernon and River Street, occupies parts of the basement, the front bay of the Meeting House proper and the belfry, extending through no less than six floors.

Theosophical Temple, Amsterdam

Temple into public library

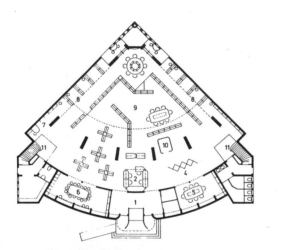

The former Theosophical Temple in the 'de Pijp' quarter of Amsterdam, built to the designs of J. Brinkman and L.C. van der Vlugt in 1927, has been converted into a branch library. The Amsterdam Theosophical Society, part of an international movement in search of the 'whole truth', wanted a functional and inexpensive building that could hold a large number of people. The architect responded with a building of unusual shape: a quarter-segment of a circle on plan, with the speaker positioned on a platform near the centre-point of the circle. For the Theosophist, truth is synonymous with light, and the need for symbolism did not go unanswered. The ceiling sloped up and the floor down to the central point, while light was directed on to the speaker through the side walls. The interior was plastered to a rough texture and painted white. The drama was heightened for the congregation by having to pass through a low and dark reception area, under the large balcony extending across the back of the hall, before entering the meeting hall proper.

Financial difficulties soon forced the Society to let the building for concerts and lectures, and during the Second World War the occupying German forces converted the building into a cinema, causing the windows to be blocked. In 1945 the Society regained their temple but continued to let it as a cinema, for which it was well suited with its sloping floor and large balcony. In 1979 – even as the neighbourhood, alarmed by plans to demolish the building, set up a committee to discuss its future – the cinema moved out and the building became temporarily a Moroccan mosque with the mullah occupying the projection room. Inspired by a student project at the Rietveld Academy, the neighbourhood committee conceived the idea of converting the building into a branch library and, furthermore, persuaded the local council to acquire the building and undertake the conversion work.

The architects for the conversion of the Theosophical Temple expressed the conflict inherent in the conversion of old buildings to new uses when they said: 'our assignment is to design a good library but we also have a responsibility towards the building that is to be preserved as a monument'. Externally, the building has been finished with the same plaster, and the roof covered with the same copper as specified by the original architects; but there have also been changes. A sloping glass wall under the roof has replaced the former balcony so that the library, quite appropriately, now opens out on to the street. For the entrance porch the architects followed the original design rather than the simplified and cheapened form that was actually built.

Internally, the lending library occupies the space of the old meeting hall, with non-fiction works in white bookcases against the walls, and fiction in black bookcases grouped informally in the middle to encourage people to meander and make their choice. Where the speaker once stood there is now a round table at which eight people can study, and to the right and left of the entrance there are semi-enclosed spaces with large tables – one designed for children and the other for reading newspapers. The old staircases have been repaired and provide access to the balcony, which has been divided by partitions into separate areas: a small meeting room on one side, a large study room with reference books and clipping files in the middle, and a workroom for the staff on the other side. The former outer balcony, now part of the interior, is both a circulation area and a place for study with its continuous desk-top and chairs. The whole building is heated by two warm air units which have been carefully hidden in the former organ space at the apex of the hall. The most impressive feature of all is the way light pours in through the long thin windows, bringing this unique space back to life.

Opposite, above: *Ground-floor plan. 1 entrance; 2 information desk; 3 catalogues; 4 exhibition area; 5 newspapers; 6 children; 7 students; 8 non-fiction; 9 fiction; 10 lift; 11 staircase. The plan form is like a slice of cake, with a round study table at the apex, where formerly the speaker stood to address his fellow Theosophists.*

Opposite, below: *The semi-enclosed children's area, situated in what, under the Theosophists, was a dark cloakroom and a place of silence, has become a bright and cosy space with colourful stools and bookcases, globe lamps and handy booktrays, from which children can select their books by the cover.*

Right: *The public reading room, with its curved balcony, sloping ceiling and tall window slits directing light forwards. At the front of the balcony are the magazines, with a conference room and study area behind. Below can be seen the open and informal arrangement of the black bookcases containing fiction, and the more closely spaced white bookcases containing non-fiction beyond. These bookcases have vertically mounted fluorescent tubes, which are shaded so that the light is thrown sideways onto the books and the visitor standing in front of the bookcase is not blinded.*

St Oswald's Old Church, Fulford, UK

Church into private house

The parlour, or former chancel, with its Norman side windows and Gothic east window. The fifteenth-century carved oak roof was rediscovered above a Victorian barrel vault and restored. The fireplace is new, but looks as if it had always been there, and the medieval floor tiles were rescued from a local archaeological excavation.

The problems encountered in the conversion of St Oswald's Old Church, Yorkshire, into a private house are typical of redundant churches generally. It took at least seven years, during which time some twenty different uses were put forward, before the present owner, Mr Roy Grant, bought the building in 1980 and began restoring and converting it. During this long period of indecision the building suffered rapid dereliction, which inevitably added considerably to the cost of restoration.

The church is dedicated to St Oswald, the Saxon king of Northumbria, and there is evidence from an archaeological investigation carried out just before the conversion works were begun, that a Saxon chapel once stood on the site. After the Norman Conquest the manor of Fulford, together with the chapel, was given by its lord to St Mary's Abbey at York, and the surviving church dates from the century following this acquisition. The nave was erected in the early part, and the chancel in the latter part, of the twelfth century. The church was never enlarged, but the Gothic east window was added around 1300, the windows on the south side were inserted during the seventeenth century, and the present brick tower replaced an earlier one in the eighteenth century. By the middle of the nineteenth century the church had become too small for the congregation, and in 1866 a large new church was built. Old St Oswald's continued to be used for occasional services until it was formally declared redundant in 1973.

Mr Grant's brief was unusual. He asked that the nave and chancel remain virtually unchanged to provide a suitable space for his collection of early oak furniture and medieval works of art. As a matter of principle it was agreed that alterations should be minimal and that any new structures within the building should be constructed in such a way that they could at any future date be dismantled without affecting the original structure.

In converting the church, the chancel has become the parlour; this involved the provision of a new floor (for damp and insulation purposes), complete with a new stone fireplace and chimneystack over. For the new floor, medieval quarry tiles, rescued in previous excavations by the York Archaeological Trust, were used. When opening up the Victorian depressed barrel vault over the chancel, the original medieval roof was discovered in a structurally unsound condition. This has been fully restored with second-hand timber.

The nave has become the dining hall, with the new balcony at the west end providing the space for a library. The area under the balcony contains the hall, flanked by the entrance lobby and stairs up to the balcony on one side, and by the bathroom on the other. Here, too, a new floor was needed and, when the 1920s timber floor was taken up, the original York stone flags were found intact underneath. They were taken up and re-laid to form the new floor.

The kitchen has been positioned in the base of the tower, and a new spiral staircase, formed in brickwork salvaged from the tower, has been constructed to serve two small bedrooms in the tower. This staircase is designed to blend with the old building, and reveals a different attitude from, say, most of the Italian examples in this book, where the new work is always very obviously new.

St Oswald's has become more than a dwelling house. It has developed into a centre for cultural activities and a meeting place for scholars and students. The building itself is a small museum of the Middle Ages and its activities seek to illustrate aspects of medieval culture.

Below, left: At the west end of the dining hall, or former nave, there is the entrance hall with a bathroom on one side and a staircase leading up to a new balcony on the other. Beyond the hall and within the tower is the kitchen.

Below, right: St Oswald's Old Church from the south, with its tower, nave and chancel seen as three distinct forms. The stone nave and chancel date from the twelfth century, though the windows are a seventeenth-century insertion, and the brick tower is eighteenth-century. The only external alteration on this side of the church is the new chimney on the chancel wall.

St James the Less, St Peter Port, Guernsey

Church into concert hall and assembly rooms

The interior of the church transformed into a concert hall. The nineteenth-century chancel, with its coffered ceiling, oak panelling and Italianate frescoes, has been restored and now provides an extension and a backdrop to the stage. On the left is one of the pine columns supporting the horseshoe balcony that provides additional seating. The upholstered chairs on the main floor of the hall can be removed to provide space for exhibitions and ceremonial events.

The Church of St James the Less was built in 1818 in the neo-classical style to the designs of the Board of Ordnance Clerk of Works, John Wilson. It is situated in a Regency suburb of Guernsey's capital, St Peter Port, which, like the church, was erected for the island's British garrison and for the English-speaking people who had taken up residence on the island following the end of hostilities with France. In the late nineteenth century a chancel with an apsidal end and coffered vault was added at the east end. By 1970 the church had become redundant and its ownership was transferred to the island government. A plan partly to demolish the church and convert it into a police station was thwarted by the Friends of St James Association, who in 1983 persuaded the authorities to pay for its restoration and conversion into concert and assembly rooms, on condition that the Association equipped, maintained and administered the building, relying on income from lettings, donations and legacies.

At its western end the church consisted of a temple front surmounted by a cylindrical steeple. Internally there was a wide rectangular nave with a horseshoe-shaped timber gallery and an arch at the eastern end forming the proscenium to the chancel beyond. The building was reasonably wind- and

The neo-classical west front of the church, with its grand pedimented entrance surmounted by a cylindrical steeple. The exterior was finished with Roman cement stucco imitating stone. This was no longer available, so matching the colour and texture where repair was needed was particularly difficult.

watertight, but had suffered from wet and dry rot and death-watch beetle. The columns supporting the gallery required new concrete foundations, the lathe-and-plaster ceiling of the nave had to be renewed, and the entire cornice replaced in fibrous plaster. The original timber-boarded and joisted floor, already partly removed on account of dry rot, was replaced with a concrete floor incorporating heating pipes to eliminate the need for unsightly radiators. To preserve the church's excellent acoustics, as much as possible of the soft lime wall plaster was retained or replaced with a comparable plaster. The panelled joinery, the gallery with its pews, the frescoes and the original furnishings and fittings were generally retained and restored or, in the case of the gas-brackets, converted to electricity.

To make the space suitable for concerts, upholstered chairs have been provided on the ground floor and the gallery pews have been deepened and also upholstered, giving a total seating capacity of 600. A recording room has been discreetly incorporated at the back of the hall. The former church hall serves rehearsal and green room needs and provides a space for smaller meetings. An artists' dressing room and administrative office are situated in a newly constructed link building between the two halls.

Hospitalet church, Ibiza

Church into art gallery and concert hall

The west front of the church after restoration. The wall has been raised, and a simple bell, visible through an opening in the wall, has replaced the former belfry. A moulding has also been introduced in the stucco around the circular window, to reconcile its off-centre position with the niche and entrance door below.

The small eighteenth-century Hospitalet church in Ibiza has been restored and altered to provide a space for exhibitions and chamber concerts, as well as religious ceremonies. By the 1970s the church had become derelict and was threatened with collapse. The restoration work was carried out between 1981 and 1984 by the Spanish Ministry of Culture and included increasing the strength of the vaults, reinforcing and re-facing the walls, and generally renovating the fabric.

The church consisted of four vaulted bays, with side chapels separated by piers. The easternmost bay formed the chancel, and a gallery in the westernmost bay was reached by a staircase winding its way through one end of the sacristy, which formed a two-storey extension on the north side of the church. In addition to the gallery and room over the sacristy, there were shallow upper galleries above the side chapels.

The west front of the church has been altered by raising the wall and substituting for the central belfry a simple bell, which is placed to one side and visible through an opening in the wall. The silhouette has therefore been modified, but the change remains within traditional patterns. The strong blue and orange colours used in the chancel, and especially in the former sacristy, are also traditional. Internally, the light passing through the round window is controlled by a sliding circular shutter that reproduces the waning phases of the moon. The sacristy has been converted on the ground floor into a new entrance, and upstairs into a dressing room.

At the east end a series of new skylights forms a fan shape under the vault. For religious services a movable altar is brought in, and the chancel wall is furnished with the former altar painting, a new canopy and tabernacle. For exhibitions and concerts these objects are covered up or folded away. The floor of large slate slabs has inlaid pieces of white marble acting as markers for exhibition panels, which can be arranged in a variety of ways.

Above: *The west front of the church before restoration, with the wall terminating in a full double slope with a central belfry rising behind.*

Right: *The nave of the church looking towards the raised chancel at the east end. The effect of the new skylights can be seen under the chancel vault and in the galleries above the side chapels. The altarpiece, baldacchino and tabernacle are open in readiness for a religious service, but they can also be folded away or covered up when the church is used for concerts or exhibitions. In its closed position the baldacchino offers a barely noticeable white back from which a boomerang shape has been cut out. As it opens, it reveals a black surface with spotlights shining from it, resembling a portion of night sky, and the cut-out is transformed into a sickle moon.*

The staircase, which starts near the entrance door, passes through the former sacristy and leads to the gallery in the westernmost bay of the church.

The white marble pieces set into the black slate floor may look like another reference to the night sky, but they serve a practical purpose, acting as markers and containing sockets for exhibition panels.

Kloster Petershausen, Constance, West Germany

Benedictine priory into multiple use

A fine space in the attic of the sixteenth-century priory (see page 9 for a plan of the whole site) which now houses the recently established Constance School of Music. The building has been made weather-tight but has otherwise not been restored or converted. A full renovation of the interior will be carried out when funds become available.

The name Petershausen derives from the ambition of the founder bishop, Gebhard II, to reproduce in architectural terms the See of Rome at Constance. A Benedictine foundation of AD 983, the priory was built on the right bank of the Rhine, just as St Peter's was built on the right bank of the Tiber, the respective cities standing on the opposite bank. Nothing is known about the first church, which burnt down in 1159. The Romanesque basilica with nave and two aisles that replaced it in 1173 survived until 1832 and is known from engravings. With the exception of a short break at the Reformation when the monks were temporarily driven out, the priory survived for over 800 years until 1802, when the Margrave of Baden made it into his palace. Converted into an army hospital during the Napoleonic Wars, it remained in the hands of the military both as barracks and hospital until 1977, when the occupying French forces finally left. Indeed, in 1877, with the growth of the German army, it had been found necessary to build a large new barracks block along the recently constructed railway line.

The historic buildings that survived were the priory, along Spanierstrasse, built between 1550 and 1630 with ceilings of wood-panel and stucco decoration; the building of the same date linking the priory to the former church; the monks' quarters, built in the form of a palace in 1769 and incorporating a refectory with rococo stucco decoration; the Torkel or wine-press building of the same date, in which nothing original survived; the 1877 barrack block, and the 1899 officers' mess on the Rhine. In 1977 all these buildings, with the exception of the Torkel, were listed in the *Land's* register of monuments, and in 1979 a national architectural competition was launched jointly by the federal and *Land* governments to find the project that would best create an administrative, social and cultural centre by converting the old buildings to new uses and by introducing new buildings, including housing, on the large areas of empty land within the site. The project awarded first prize was adopted, and work began in 1981, with two-thirds of the money coming from the federal and *Land* governments, and one-third from the private sector.

The large site was full of shacks and sheds, most of which have now been cleared. The officers' mess was taken over as early as 1979 by the Lake of Constance Symphony Orchestra for its administration and rehearsals without the need for a major restoration. Similarly, the newly created School of Music moved into the priory in 1984 without carrying out any conversion work beyond making the building weatherproof. A major renovation of the interior awaits finance that the School at present lacks. The monks' quarters, on the other hand, have been fully restored and converted to receive the city archives and museum; and the Torkel building has been renewed internally to accommodate ancillary local government offices and a high school. Immediately to the west of the Torkel building the main local government offices are housed in a large, new, three-storey block, planned around three courtyards with an internal street running through the middle. This and the two recently completed housing blocks to the north of the 1877 barrack block were the subject of further architectural competitions and have been successfully integrated into the historic site.

The conversion of the 1877 barrack block into the police headquarters and a series of new buildings along Petershausenstrasse, containing shops at street level and flats above and behind, will be completed by 1992, as will the landscaping of the considerable areas of open space to provide a small public park, several tree-lined streets and car parking concealed by planting. So far only the courtyard landscaping directly related to the new buildings and the Benediktinerplatz opposite the Torkel building has been completed. The last new building, to be constructed to the west of the monks' quarters some time after 1992, will be a concert hall, but this will sadly require the demolition of the existing nineteenth-century housing blocks west of the priory and the re-routing of Spanierstrasse. Like the City Hall block in Helsinki (p. 18), Petershausen is an excellent example of how conversion of an entire complex of redundant buildings can be staggered to ease the burden of finance.

The eighteenth-century monks' quarters before and after restoration. The building has been converted into the city archives and museum.

Charterhouse of Ittingen, Thurgau, Switzerland

Carthusian monastery into multiple use

The Charterhouse of Ittingen was founded in 1461, when the Carthusian monks took over an impoverished Augustinian priory which had been in existence for over 300 years. The buildings that have survived date from the reconstruction of the monastery in the sixteenth century, following a fire at the time of the Reformation, and mainly from the seventeenth and eighteenth centuries. With its wonderful baroque church by Caspar Moosbrugger, the Charterhouse is of European importance, and its future therefore became a matter of great concern when the family, who had bought the property some time after the last monks had left in 1848, decided they could no longer look after it. Fortunately, in 1977 the newly established Foundation Charterhouse Ittingen bought the buildings and carried out an imaginative conversion, which was completed in 1983. The Charterhouse is now the Thurgau Cultural Centre and includes the Ittingen Museum of History and the Art Museum, both run by the canton; a conference centre with its hotel; a social centre and hostel; a restaurant and banqueting hall; and the church itself, superbly restored and used for recitals, but also for religious services.

The nucleus of the monastery consisted of two adjacent courtyards. The small cloister was surrounded by monastic ranges on the west, south and east sides, containing the prior's lodgings, the refectories, the chapter house and sacristy, and by the church itself on the north side. The large cloister was

Above: *The Charterhouse of Ittingen seen from the vineyard slopes which rise to the north of the monastery. The view shows the large cloister, with the church on the right and the monks' cells in the form of little gable-ended houses on the far side and left. On the near side, where the monastery was open to the hill, a series of new buildings of similar form to the monks' cells provide exhibition galleries for the art museum.*

Right: *The gloriously ornate high altar of the restored church, built between 1763 and 1767 in marblized stucco by Johann Georg Gigl, with applied wood carving by Matthias Faller.*

surrounded on the south and east sides by monks' cells in the form of small, gable-ended houses, each containing a workshop, ambulatory, living room, box bed and prayer room, where the monk could pursue the hermit's existence ordained by St Bruno, the eleventh-century founder of the order. On the north side the court was open to the hill that rises steeply at the foot of the monastery. This gap has been closed with new buildings that take the same form as the monks' cells, providing a long gallery, with a series of lofty exhibition halls off it, for the Art Museum. The existing buildings surrounding the two cloisters have been restored and converted into the Ittingen Museum of History.

To the west of this monastic nucleus was appended a very large court surrounded by service buildings and stores, which included granary, mill, bakehouse, dairy, barns and stables. The granary and mill have been converted into a bar and restaurant; the stables into workshops; the fine cellars underneath into a banqueting hall; and the barns into a hostel and social centre. Where the dairy once stood in the north-west corner, two new ranges have been built to accommodate a small hotel and conference centre. These buildings have high roofs and are generally traditional in form and in the materials they use, but in detail and in the way the materials are put together they are unmistakably of today.

One of the exhibition galleries of the art museum. It is open to the roof, but a flat ceiling is suspended over part of the space to bring down the height.

Rural Buildings

Farmhouse

Barn

Granary

Hunting lodge

Menagerie

The adult library in a converted farmhouse at Hospitalet de Llobregat, near Barcelona, consists of several long, narrow reading rooms with low ceilings, providing an appropriately intimate atmosphere. The reading table and integral lamp were specially designed and are a standard fitting used by the Catalonian library service throughout all its buildings.

Like churches, barns and granaries are composed of a shell enclosing a large single volume, sometimes divided horizontally by a floor, to which subsidiary spaces have often been added. Unlike churches, though, this shell is an unadorned structure meeting the demands of function in a simple and direct manner. Because barns and granaries were intended for the storage of goods, they rarely have any windows, and openings are limited to large doors at ground level and, occasionally, loading doors at a high level with hoisting machinery above. The farm cottage at Wantage (p.196), for example, had hoisting machinery incorporated in the form of a wooden windlass when it was raised by a floor in 1790 to turn it into a cloth-dyeing workshop.

Though the simplicity and solidity of rural buildings would appear to make them ideal subjects for conversion, barns and granaries do, nevertheless, present their own characteristic difficulties. The absence in this chapter of any conversions to domestic use is due to the difficulty of turning a barn into a house without depriving it of its distinctive marks. A house almost inevitably requires subdivision of the space and the introduction of windows and doors, whereas an office, museum or workshop, examples of which are illustrated here, can keep the space as one and can rely to a much greater extent on artificial light. The conversion at Hadleigh in Suffolk (p.206), of a granary and four houses into the local council's offices, is especially noteworthy because a group of old buildings that formed an integral part of the historic town has been saved and given new life, where otherwise the group would have been replaced by a single, large new building.

In selecting examples for this section it was felt especially important that the building should have retained its character after conversion. No significant examples could be found in America, France or Italy. In my experience, barns in France and Italy are still very much in agricultural use. In Germany, on the other hand, examples are plentiful, but conversions tend to be so radical that the buildings are transformed, losing their original character. Such is the case with the seventeenth-century royal stables at Sankt Blasien, which have been converted to provide additional accommodation for a convalescent home, consisting of leisure rooms, offices, a travel agency, an assembly hall and foyer, and a local museum. At Darmsheim the local authority has converted the sixteenth-century half-timbered tithe barn into a club house for local choral, music and theatre societies, but not without subdividing the lofty space of the barn by the insertion of additional floors. Only in the loft, where the multi-purpose hall is exposed to the oak roof trusses, does the rugged character of the barn survive. At Neukirchen, however, the conversion of another tithe barn into a church and community centre suggests a more sympathetic new use. Indeed, the only example of note in France is also a tithe barn, a particularly magnificent thirteenth-century example originally at La Neuville-du-Bosc. It was dismantled, moved and re-erected in 1969 at the Benedictine abbey of Saint-Wandrille in Normandy, where it became the abbey church, the French Revolution having reduced the medieval church to ruins. The stone barn has a grand structure of elm posts and trusses, which form a well-defined nave and two aisles. It makes a wonderful, if unconventional church.

The moving of barns in this way is a relatively common, but controversial practice. The barn may be removed from the site for which it was originally intended, but, on the other hand, this may be the only way to safeguard its continued existence and to bring new life to a redundant but historically important building. In the case of the late elm barn that now forms part of the

The magnificent thirteenth-century tithe barn which was moved from La Neuville-du-Bosc to the Benedictine abbey of Saint-Wandrille in Normandy, where it now serves as the abbey church. The interior shows the grand elm structure of posts and trusses, and illustrates how the division of the space into a nave and two aisles made it an obvious candidate for conversion into a church.

The Court Hill Youth Hostel and Ridgeway Centre at Wantage consists of five redundant barns which were dismantled and re-erected on a site high on the edge of the Berkshire Downs.

Vale and Downland Museum at Wantage, Oxfordshire, the brain-child of Dr Richard Squires, the various parts of the weatherboarded barn were labelled before being dismantled, and it was then re-erected on new brick foundations and oak wall plates. In a museum, exhibits are often best lit by artificial light alone, so no windows were required and the integrity of the barn was preserved. Another of Dr Squires' projects involved five redundant local barns, which were dismantled and brought to a site high on the edge of the Berkshire Downs. Here they were re-erected on piled foundation slabs in the form of a traditional farm. They are now the Court Hill Youth Hostel and Ridgeway Centre. The main barn provides the dining room and kitchen; the open cow byre, stabling for horses and storage for bicycles and tents; while the other barns provide sleeping accommodation for more than 60, field-study facilities, a warden's house and two holiday flats.

Also in the Wantage area, the tireless Dr Squires has found new uses for the Lains Barn, a group of farm buildings that includes a large barn, dating in part from 1750, and an L-shaped cow byre enclosing a fold yard. These were restored and converted for community and educational use, leaving the majestic spaces intact. The low-key conversion was carried out mainly with voluntary labour and old materials, and is considered one of the most successful barn conversions in Britain.

Equally successful is the conversion of the great barn at Froidmont in Belgium into a church for the Dominican monks who took over the historic farmstead in the mid-1970s. With the help of Lucien Kroll, a pioneer of community architecture, the monks carried out the conversion work without compromising the single volume of the barn or sacrificing its character, even though galleries were added. The monks have also converted the remaining buildings, which are grouped round a large farmyard, into parish rooms, seminar rooms, living cells and a library, and have built a new range of maisonettes for letting to the local community.

Less sophisticated and emphatically rustic in character are the fine interiors of a group of late eighteenth-century farm buildings at Kruh in Czechoslovakia. These have been restored and converted into a recreation centre for the Faculty of Architecture of the Technical University in Prague, and now consist of a dining hall and kitchen, guest rooms, social rooms and a few offices.

The lesson to be learnt from these conversions of rural buildings is twofold: that the integrity of the space and structure of a barn or granary must be fully respected, and that the new materials and finishes introduced must be in sympathy with the character of the building. To follow these principles when converting rural buildings inevitably imposes limitations and restricts the type of use to one that requires the minimum of change, but the examples that follow show how, even within these parameters, successful transformations can be achieved.

Old Surgery, Wantage, UK

Farm cottage and barn into local museum

The new double-height extension at the back of the Old Surgery is in use as a coffee bar. The roof structure of curved laminated beams recalls traditional cruck construction.

The conversion of the Old Surgery at Wantage in Oxfordshire and the relocation of a Downland barn on the land behind to create a local museum was the brain-child of Dr Richard Squires, who has combined a passion for saving old barns and converting them to new uses with the busy life of a general practitioner. The building was originally a post-and-truss farm cottage, with a massive internal chalk chimneystack. In 1790 it was 'modernized' to fit its new role as a cloth-dyeing workshop, the timber-framed façade being replaced by brickwork. The roof was raised to form a large storage attic where the bales of cloth were winched from the delivery carts by means of a wooden windlass that still survives. It was used as the doctor's surgery from mid-Victorian times until the mid-1970s, when medical work was transferred to the new health centre. It was then acquired by the local authority to be converted into the town museum. For this purpose it was leased to the Vale and Downland Trust, who raised the money for the conversion and are now responsible for the day-to-day management of the museum.

The work was carried out in two stages. First, the Old Surgery was converted to provide a new entrance and two exhibition rooms on the ground floor, and offices for the administration of the museum on the first floor. At the back, directly accessible from the entrance, is a new double-height extension with a roof structure of curved laminated beams recalling traditional cruck construction. This space, which has large windows overlooking the courtyard garden at the back, forms the heart of the museum and is used for meetings, displays and films, and as a coffee bar. The first-floor gallery is for exhibitions by the local art and craft school, and also at first-floor level the manager's office projects into the space and, with its window, acts as a look-out.

The second stage consisted of re-erecting three bays of a five-bay aisled barn and building a new gallery link in an L-shape at the back of the courtyard. This appropriately houses the collection of agricultural equipment, the farm waggons and a locally made threshing machine. It is hoped eventually to acquire the adjacent site and to complete the courtyard by extending the barn.

The moving of barns in this way could be considered by some to be rather controversial. Relocating buildings goes against good conservation practice because the building is likely to suffer damage and is given a new setting for which it was never intended. In this particular instance, however, it could be argued that the barn itself becomes part of the history that the museum sets out to illustrate, acting as a 'living' exhibit.

The new extension seen from the garden behind the Old Surgery. A terrace for summer use has been formed between the extension and the garden, which is at a higher level and reached by a short flight of brick steps. On the right is the new gallery which links the old building to the relocated barn at the back of the garden.

Leatheringsett Hill, Holt, UK

Tithe barn into workshop, showroom and office

A symmetrical group of three barns around a courtyard. In converting the barns into a joinery works, a small weatherboarded extension has been built to link the central barn with the left-hand barn. There were restrictions on altering the external appearance of the barns, but on the courtyard side framed panels of glass and diagonal cedar boarding were allowed in the large openings.

English tithe barns were built for the purpose of storing taxes paid in kind by tenants to their landlords. At Letheringsett Hill in Norfolk a more ordinary barn existed on the present site from about 1800, but in 1851 this was given its spacious porch and enlarged into a symmetrical group of three barns around a courtyard. The barns had pantile roofs and flint walls with brick quoins and surrounds to the openings. The owner was the Church of England, and the rector of the time, who enjoyed the living of Holt, exacted taxes from his tenants and collected them in the tithe barn. Later, the building served various purposes of a more strictly agricultural kind, until the change in farming methods rendered it useless and caused its neglect and final abandonment.

When Mr P.H. Roberts, a local cabinet-maker whose business was expanding, acquired the barns in 1986, he found them in an advanced state of disrepair and partly collapsed. He persuaded the local planning authority to let him restore the buildings and turn them into a home for traditional wood-working. There were severe restrictions on altering their external appearance, but on the courtyard side these restrictions were somewhat relaxed, allowing large openings to be fitted with framed panels of glass and diagonal cedar boarding. The porch had to be taken down and rebuilt, as it was in an advanced state of dereliction, and a small weatherboarded extension, incorporated adroitly into the existing structure so that it looks as if it had always been there, provides a link between the main barn and one of the side barns where there was none before. The earth floors were dug out and concrete was laid throughout to enable the barns to assume their new functions: the main barn has become the workshop, one side barn serves as machine room, the other as showroom, with the separate space at the end reserved for French polishing.

Externally, the restoration of the flint walls and pantile roofs has been carried out so skilfully that it is only noticeable to the expert eye, and viewed from the road side, the barns appear virtually unaltered. Following the official opening of the barns in July 1987, the scheme received a number of awards, all of which drew attention to the way in which a simple piece of rural architecture had been restored with great sympathy and put to an industrial use that is more appropriate to its original function than a commercial use.

Above: *The workshop in the main central barn, where a gallery has been inserted at one end. From the road side (right) the barns appear virtually unaltered, their pantile roofs and flint walls with brick quoins and surrounds to the openings carefully restored. Only the porch, considered an essential feature, was sufficiently derelict to require taking down and rebuilding.*

Hospitalet de Llobregat, Barcelona, Spain

Barn and farmhouse into public library

Hospitalet de Llobregat is an expanding dormitory town on the coast west of Barcelona. In an effort to provide this sprawling conglomeration of tall apartment blocks with amenities, the Catalonian library service decided to convert a seventeenth-century farmstead into a public library for 180 readers and 36,000 volumes. The farmstead, which was a gift to the town from its last occupant, Dr Prats, consisted of a house and a barn facing one another across a courtyard and connected by walls. On the far side of the house was another walled courtyard.

In converting the buildings the architects have introduced new elements. These will be criticized by conservationists who prefer old buildings to be altered as little as possible, but they seem wholly appropriate both to the new function and to the existing random rubble and roughly stuccoed walls that determine the character of the place. The paved and landscaped courtyard becomes the entrance and the hub of the complex. From it one enters the children's library (formerly the barn) as well as the adult library (formerly the house). Both buildings have had their roofs extended and supported on large circular concrete columns. In the case of the children's library, the space under the roof is now a shady loggia with a long bench. Here the entrances into the courtyard and into the children's library are found. For the adult library the space under the roof has been glazed and contains the entrance lobby and a ramp to the upper floor. Inside, it consists of several long narrow reading rooms with low ceilings, the larger of which give on to the other walled courtyard, while the children's library has had galleries added, with a rooflight along the ridge.

This conversion is one of several resulting from the Catalonian library service's policy of increasing the number of public libraries. To do this

Both farmhouse and barn have had their roofs extended to provide loggias on the courtyard side. These loggias form the entrances, and in the case of the farmhouse (now the adult library) on the far side of the courtyard (right) *the space has been glazed and contains a ramp from the entrance lobby to the first floor. The barn has been converted into the children's library* (opposite). *Into the double-height space have been inserted two high-level galleries which provide additional floor area and at the same time bring down the ceiling height at the edges. Continuous roof glazing on either side of the ridge floods the library with light.*

The ramp leading up to the first floor in the adult library (left) and one of the reading rooms in the adult library with a view on to its own quiet courtyard (above).

The roof extension to the children's library, with its supporting circular concrete columns, becomes an open, but shaded loggia as well as an entrance porch.

quickly it was decided to make use of old buildings and to develop a range of standard furniture and fixtures. A system of adjustable shelves and display racks was devised, and a reading table designed. Lighting is integral, with strips fixed to the top of the shelves for general illumination and a table lamp for the individual reader.

Stone barn, St Andrew, Guernsey

Barn into architects' offices

When BASA Architects outgrew their offices, they decided to design for themselves accommodation that would not only meet their design standards, but also reflect the practice's conservation philosophy. In 1986 a derelict stone barn that appeared to meet all their basic needs became available at St Andrew in Guernsey. The conversion work began in April 1987 and was finished seven months later. The barn has a high spacious interior, which allowed the introduction of an upper-floor design studio lit through rooflights along the lower slopes of the barn roof. The north–south orientation of the building ensured good natural lighting conditions over each drawing board, and the end window in the north gable now provides long-distance views of the west coast through the upper leaves and branches of the tree growing in the courtyard below, which has been paved with brick and cobblestones.

The ground floor provides for the general administration requirements of the practice. A reception area, containing screened work stations for the administrative staff, leads directly from the entrance courtyard and gives access to a conference room, partners' office and accommodation for the two chartered building surveyors employed by the practice.

The granite barn converted into architects' offices. A row of roof-lights has been fitted into the pantile roof to light the upper-floor design studio, which has been built within the existing structure.

The interior and exterior retain the character of the nineteenth-century barn. Instead of rainwater pipes, heavy chains are used to bring the water to the ground, in the Japanese fashion. Wherever possible existing building materials from the site have been used in the reconstruction, so that much of the original patina of the structure has been preserved, mitigating the impact of the more modern additions, such as the roof-lights.

The external granite walls of the building were not in good condition and were incapable of withstanding the additional thrust imposed on them by the new upper floor. The loading on the walls has been reduced considerably by the introduction internally of oak posts rising the full height of the building and supporting beams carrying both the upper floor and the roof. The oak posts, beams and roof trusses are all left exposed in their natural state and, together with the pointed granite walls and coarse-textured, natural fibre fitted carpet, make an appropriate addition to the rude interior. The clean lines of well-designed modern furniture, screens, office equipment and brightly coloured door furniture complement and contrast with the natural quality of the structural elements.

The reception area on the ground floor where the administration is housed. To support the new upper floor and to take the load of the roof trusses from the decrepit granite walls, a new oak structure of posts and beams has been introduced. The curves and clean lines of the bespoke furniture provide a contrast to the rough texture of wood and stone.

Malthouse granary, Hadleigh, UK

Granary and houses into council offices

The nineteenth-century malthouse granary, which takes up a whole side of the principal courtyard, has been converted into two floors of open offices, the upper floor reaching into the roof space (above). The public enter through one of the old houses into the principal court (opposite). On the left is the octagonal waiting room, and beyond, the conservatory, which wraps round the council chamber on the courtyard side; at the far end of the courtyard stands the malthouse granary.

After the reorganization of English local government in 1974, a number of the newly formed local authorities built themselves large new council offices, usually on the outskirts of the town. Operating from Hadleigh, a historic town of outstanding quality, Babergh District Council in Suffolk decided otherwise, and created their new headquarters (opened in 1982) out of a nucleus of old buildings.

The site overlooks the River Brett in what is still Constable country and includes a nineteenth-century malthouse granary and four houses, all of which are listed as buildings of special architectural and historic interest. They had become partly derelict and the ground around was untended and in a poor state of repair. They have been converted and connected with five new buildings to form a series of landscaped courtyards and the new headquarters can now house the six departments of the council, which is served by a staff of more than two hundred.

At the centre is the new octagonal council chamber, from which a number of routes radiate to the different departments and cafeteria. The public enter through the small doorway of one of the old houses to find an octagonal waiting room reminiscent of a garden pavilion behind the house. The public routes through the building are pleasantly informal, and people can linger in the conservatory that wraps round the council chamber on the courtyard side, in the cafeteria, or – in good weather – on the terrace outside.

The new buildings have massive hipped roofs with continuous windows under the eaves but, in the case of the large administration block, the bulk is broken down by the stepped section with its upper and lower roof separated by a clerestory. Over the pantiled roofs rises the slate roof of the council chamber, dominating the group. In the new, as in the old, the materials are

The council chamber has its ceiling and walls covered in horizontal cedar boarding. It is octagonal in plan and has a high pyramidal roof which dominates the group.

mostly brick and timber, with the council chamber's ceiling and walls covered in horizontal cedar boards.

Babergh District Council covers a considerable area, so good car-parking facilities were essential. The solution has been to place the 85-space car park out of sight on the far side of the river and to connect it with the council offices by a new footbridge.

208

The ground floor of the converted malthouse granary has cast-iron columns supporting heavy beams, which in turn support the joists of the upper floor.

Chatelherault, Hamilton, UK

Hunting lodge and visitors' centre

Chatelherault, the former hunting lodge and garden pavilion of the Dukes of Hamilton, was built between 1732 and 1743 to the designs of William Adam (father of Robert and John). It has been restored thanks to the British government's acceptance of the property in lieu of death duties and to Hamilton District Council's agreement to take the buildings over after restoration and convert them into a centre for the Chatelherault County Park. Chatelherault, which William Adam referred to as a 'Dogg Kennel', terminated the vista from Hamilton Palace, the largest private house in Scotland, which was demolished in the 1920s. The ground originally rose steadily all the way to the hunting lodge, which was joined to the palace by a mile-long double avenue of trees.

In recent years, however, these Grade A listed buildings and garden terraces had reached the last stages of dereliction, racked by mining settlement, set on fire, vandalized and rendered largely roofless and floorless. Extensive sand quarrying had radically reduced the level of the ground on the north, east and west sides, and the buildings themselves would have been destroyed for the sand underneath them, but for the fact that the district council refused planning permission.

The buildings consisted of two groups of pavilions. The eastern pavilions, which were partly stables, partly houses for estate workers, screened a large court containing the kennels, the game larder, washhouse, dairy, stores, etc. The western pavilions formed a series of magnificently decorated rooms for the use of the Duke and his family. They included a banqueting hall that opened, by a Venetian window, on to a formal parterre garden with, beyond, a splendid terrace walk.

The restoration took eight years and was completed in 1987. For the stonework the original Deer Park quarry within 100 yards of the buildings was re-opened. A new circular stone staircase conceals an underground storage and service area, and tidies up what had become a hotch-potch of accretions behind the central screen wall. The plaster decoration by Thomas Clayton (1710–60) had largely disappeared. Only in the Duke's room had parts of it been taken down and stored, and a full photographic record made. An

The entrance front before restoration. It is this side of the hunting lodge which terminated the mile-long vista from Hamilton Palace. The east pavilions on the left were partly stables and partly houses for estate workers. The houses have been restored, and the stables converted into a tourist shop and into additional accommodation for the houses. The west pavilions, which contained a series of grand rooms for the use of the duke and his family, have been restored and can be let for functions.

The upper floor of the duke's apartment in the west pavilions before and after restoration. Only in the duke's room had parts of the plasterwork been taken down and stored, and a full photographic record made.

The new circular stone staircase (top) *conceals an underground storage and service area, and tidies up what had become a hotch-potch of accretions behind the central wall which joins the west and east pavilions* (above).

The banqueting hall in the west pavilions (opposite) *opens with a Venetian window on to the parterre garden, which has been authentically restored.*

experiment in restoring the Duke's apartment, by taking parts of the surviving fragments and preparing full-size drawings, was so successful that it was extended to the banqueting hall on the basis of photographs only. The new plasterwork, by Leonard Stead of Bradford, was modelled and cast off-site and then fixed to strapping, unlike Clayton's, which was applied direct to the stone and modelled in situ.

The conversion work included the construction of a new entrance and roadway across the front, and car parks to the east and west, one of which is concealed in the old sand workings. The former kennel courtyard, with its conglomeration of out-buildings, has been rebuilt to provide a visitor centre with a new exhibition area and auditorium. The central part of the eastern pavilions has been altered internally to provide an entrance for the public and a shop, where there had been stabling for four horses and sculleries. A former hayloft has been turned into bedrooms and bathrooms for the houses that flank the shop. Within the western pavilions, structural alterations were necessary to provide circulation and lavatories in the basement vaults, so that the five rooms could be let for functions or visited for their own sake. The terrace gardens and their heavily damaged walls have been repaired, and the parterre garden has been authentically restored following an extensive archaeological dig.

The Menagerie, Horton, UK

Menagerie into private residence

The plan of the Menagerie (below) is oriented northwards in the direction of the great house, to which it belonged. This side was built of stone, whereas the south side facing the zoo was built of brick and had no windows. The plan shows the remodelling of the south side with its two new end pavilions duplicating the original end pavilions on the north side. All new work is shown hatched.

The dining room (opposite) is an entirely new space created behind what was only a stone screen linking the saloon with one of the end pavilions. The view shows the steps up to the saloon.

From Horton House, Northamptonshire, demolished between the Wars, it was about a mile and a half across the park to the Menagerie, where the second Earl of Halifax would bring his guests to luncheon and to view the animals and birds in his private zoo, housed in a circular enclosure at the back of the building. The Menagerie, superbly restored and now converted by Mr Gervase Jackson-Stops into a house for himself, dates from the 1750s. It is one of the most important surviving works of the architect, astronomer and garden-designer Thomas Wright of Durham, who also made alterations to Horton House and advised on the layout of the park and on the garden buildings round its perimeter.

The central block of the Menagerie contained one very large room where luncheon – prepared in the brick-vaulted cellar below – would have been served. The two pavilions at either end were probably used for storing gardening tools and food for the animals. The walls that linked them to the central block were only screens, with gateways in the central arches leading to the zoo. This northern side of the building, with its remarkable silhouette, was the only important façade, being the side visible from the main house; it was built of stone, whereas the side facing the zoo was built of brick and had no windows. The style of the building, with its split pediment, rusticated windows with balustrades below them, and niches with prominent keystones, is essentially Palladian, as had been practised by William Kent and Lord Burlington 30 years earlier.

By 1975 the Menagerie was derelict, having been used by troops in the Second World War and continually vandalized in the following years. The pyramidal roofs over the end pavilions had been replaced by flat corrugated iron sheets and the half-dome over the bay, by an ugly three-pitch roof, while in the great central room about half of the marvellous decorative plasterwork had disappeared.

The initial restoration began in 1975. The central portico on the south façade (there is evidence that this may have been the only decorative feature on this side of the building) was not completed until 1988. The sash windows on either side of this central feature were inserted during the initial restoration, but the wings enlarging the dining room and adding two bedrooms were built between 1980 and 1982. The end pavilions had side elevations with blind windows, which have been opened up to form proper

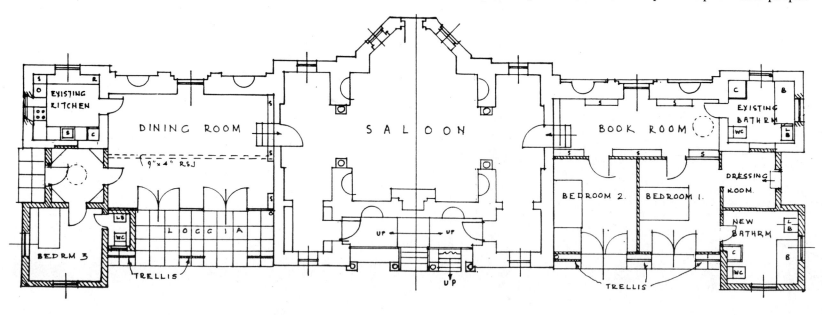

The north front before (above), *and after* (top) *restoration, with the original lead semi-dome over the central bay and the finials on the pavilions copied in fibreglass. The plinths and stone balls over the two arches have been reinstated, as has the grass mound providing a plinth for the central bay. The only change is to the two arches, where round-headed windows have replaced the original gates.*

In the great saloon (opposite) *the decorative plasterwork has been superbly restored. The deep cove of the central section is decorated with medallions of the signs of the Zodiac, presided over by Father Time, the Four Winds and the mask of Apollo in a sunburst in the ceiling above.*

windows. These pavilions have been duplicated on the south side to provide a third bedroom at one end and a bathroom at the other. The recessed link between the pavilions contains, at one end, the front door and, at the other, a round-headed window, lighting a dressing room. The east and west elevations of the new pavilions have been rendered to blend in with the stone, but also to distinguish the old work from the new. On the south side they are of random diapered brick to match the south façade. The round-headed gateways on the north façade have been filled in with windows to light the dining room and the book room.

The plasterwork in the great room has been restored by the artist and sculptor Christopher Hobbs, where freehand plasterwork was necessary, and by Leonard Stead and Son of Bradford, where the work could be done from moulds. Not surprisingly, perhaps, for an architect who was also an astronomer, the subject matter is the Zodiac, which must also have been considered suitable decoration for a menagerie because so many of the signs are represented by animals. Only two small changes were made to the great room: a pair of doors was added leading to the dining room and book room; and the south-facing sash windows already mentioned were introduced in the alcoves on either side of the chimneypiece. The result is a triumph of restoration and adaptation, and the grandest bungalow in the world.

Guide to the Schemes

Public Buildings

City Hall block, Helsinki
Client Helsinki City Council   *Architect* Professor Aarno
Ruusuvuori, architect SAFA   *Interior designers* Lauri Anttila,
Anna Jäämeri-Ruusuvuori, Raija Olsson   *Designer of relief on
wall of council chamber* Juhana Blomstedt

Gare d'Orsay, Paris
Client Ministère de la Culture   *Architects* A.C.T.
Architecture: R. Bardon, P. Colboc, J. P. Phillippon
Architect/Interior designer Gae Aulenti   *Structural engineers*
B.E.F.S. Engineering, Cabinet Ducroux et Marty,
G.E.R.I.A.C. Groupe européen   *Chief architect for historic
monuments* Michel Jantzen

Union Station, St Louis, USA
Client St Louis Station Associates   *Developer/Manager* The
Rouse Company of Missouri, Inc.   *Architects* Hellmuth,
Obata & Kassabaum, Inc.   *General contractor* HCB
Contractors, St Louis

Hospital de San Rafael, Santander, Spain
Client Regional Assembly of Cantabria   *Architects* José
Manuel Sanz Sanz, Juan Lopez Rioboo-Latorre   *Structural
engineer* Gonzalo Iglesias

Free Hospital for Women, Boston, USA
Clients Myerson/Allen and Company   *Architects* CBT/
Childs, Bertman, Tseckares & Casendino Inc.

Ospizio di San Michele, Rome
Client Ministry of Culture   *Architects for conservation*
Francesco de Tomasso, Patrizia Marchetti   *Supervising the
work* Francesco de Tomasso   *Architects for conference centre*
Franco Minissi, Gaetano Miarelli Mariani   *Superintending
engineer* Giovanni di Geso   *Structural engineers* Leopoldo
Baruchello, Amedeo Coccia, Ivo Cosimelli, Tommaso
Mazzetti

Corn Exchange, Cambridge, UK
Client Cambridge City Council   *Architects* Hamilton
Associates

Vartiovuori Observatory, Turku, Finland
Client City of Turku   *City architect* Pentti Tala
Architect for conversion Pekka Aho   *Project manager* Pentti
Saari   *Structural engineer* Veikko Mäntynen   *Builders*
Building construction department of the City of Turku
Engineers' Office

Courthouses, Cambridge, USA
Client Bulfinch Square Limited Partnership   *Architects*
Graham Gund Associates, Inc: Graham Gund, Peter
Madsen, David Perry   *Project associate* Franklyn
Lucas   *Consultants* Carol Johnson and Associates
(landscape); LeMessurier Associates SCI
(structural)   *General contractor* Erland Construction Inc.

Les Pâquis School, Geneva, Switzerland
Client/Owner Municipality of Geneva   *Architect* Ugo Brunoni,
SIA   *Collaborating architect* J.-Y. Ravier   *Structural engineers*
Liechti & Serex, SIA   *Artist/Painter (trompe-l'oeil on the first
floor)* Pierre Montant

Varney School, Manchester, USA
Funded by New Hampshire Housing Finance Agency
Architects John Sharratt Associates Inc.

Private Buildings

Castello di Rivoli, Turin, Italy
Client Region of Piemonte   *Architect* Andrea
Bruno   *Structural engineer* Franco Borini, Figli & C.
S.p.A.   *Contractor* Borini Costruzioni S.p.A.   *Painter of
ceiling vault* Antonio Carena

Castello Guidi, Vinci, Italy
Client Town council of Vinci   *Architect* Fausto
Colombo   *Consultants* Ferruccio Dragoni, Marcello Antozzi,
Augusto Marinoni

Palazzo della Pilotta, Parma, Italy
Client City of Parma   *Architect* Guido Canali

Ibrahim Pasha Palace, Istanbul
Client Ministry of Culture and Tourism, Turkey   *Architect*
Hüsrev Tayla

Qajar Palace, Tehran
Client Museum of Glass and Ceramics   *Architect* Hans
Hollein   *Project architects* Franz Madl, Gerhard Knoettig,
Gustava Leland, Jerzy Surwillo   *Structural engineers* Eckart
Dittbern & Partner   *Contractor* G.U. GmbH München,
Karl-Gerhard Hinderink

Hôtel Salé, Paris
Client City of Paris   *Architect* Roland Simounet

Benham Park, Newbury, UK
Client Norsk Data Ltd   *Architects* Niels Torp, Harald Heie,
Oddvar Johansen   *Structural engineer* Arne Hill AB, Trigram
Design Partnership   *Landscape* Bauer Karon AB   *Project
manager* Ake Larson Construction Ltd, Arnold Norvell
Management contractors John Langrind, Morris Michelsen,
Soren Wennerholm, Ron Loveridge, Goran Regnell

Gunton Hall, Cromer, UK
Client Kit Martin   *Architect* Kit Martin   *Built by* direct labour

Commercial Buildings

Palais Ferstel, Vienna
Architects Alois Machatschek, Wilfried Schermann
Architectural consultant Hans Peter Frohlich   *Structural
engineer* Peter Kotzian   *Contractors* Walter Hold, Lenikus
Ges. m.b.H.

Dairy Depot, London
Client Pentagram Design Limited   *Architects* Theo Crosby of
Pentagram, Brian Richards   *Contractor* Wates Special Works

Halles de Schaerbeek, Brussels
Clients Commission Française de la Culture de
l'Agglomération Bruxelloise (C.F.C.); Le Ministère de la
Communauté Française de Belgique   *Architect*
COOPARCH s.c.r.l.   *Project architect* Jean de
Salle   *Structural engineers* Ingénieurs Associés s.p.r.l.

Halles de l'Ile, Geneva, Switzerland
Client Municipal council of the Town of Geneva
Architect Gilbert Frey   *Civil engineer* Fol & Duchemin
SIA   *Contractor* Service immobilier de la Ville de Genève

Albert Dock, Liverpool, UK
Clients Tate Gallery, Property Services Agency
Architects James Stirling, Michael Wilford & Associates
Site supervision Holford Associates/Stirling Wilford
Associates   *Project management* D.O.E. Property Services
Agency   *Structural engineer* W. G. Curtin & Partners
Contractor Tarmac Construction

Dock Traffic Office, Liverpool, UK
Client Granada Television   *Architects* Building Design
Partnership   *Job partner* R. J. Chapman   *Structural engineer*
Greg Nolan

Kulturmagasinet, Sundsvall, Sweden
Client County council of Sundsvall   *Architect* Esse Fahlman
of the Riksbyggen Konsult studio   *Landscape design*
Riksbyggen Konsult   *Interior design* Carlbrand Macris, Jean
Carlbrand, Peter Tillberg   *Contractor* Bystroms Bygg AB

Pavillon de l'Arsenal, Paris
Client Direction de l'Aménagement Urbain de la Ville de
Paris   *Architect* Reichen et Robert   *Contractor* Rontaix

Dry-goods warehouse, Galveston, USA
Client George and Cynthia Mitchell   *Architect* Ford, Powell &
Carson, Inc.   *Landscape architect* Ford, Powell & Carson, Inc.
Interior designer Ann Milligan Gray, Inc.C.   *Contractor/
Construction manager* R & M Construction Company

South Street Seaport, New York
Clients South Street Seaport Museum; Rouse & Co.
(Development Firm); City and State of New York   *Architect*
Benjamin Thompson & Associates   *Architects and planners*
Beyer Blinder Belle (museum block and Bogardus building);
Jan Hird Pokorny (Schermerhorn Row block)

East Brother Lighthouse, San Francisco Bay, USA
Client East Brother Light Station, Inc.   *Finance* Grants from
US Department of the Interior, and many local people and
companies   *Built by* over 300 volunteers including the
California Conservation Corps

Industrial Buildings

Lowell Mills and Boott Mills, Lowell, USA
Textile mill:
Client/Developers Market Mills Associates, Lowell Historic
Preservation Commission   *Architects* Notter, Finegold,
Alexander (housing); Architectural Endevor (commercial food
court, artist); National Park Service (visitor center)
Patrick J. Mogan Cultural Center:
Developers Lowell Historic Preservation Commission, Lowell
National Historic Park   *Architect* Perry, Dean and Rogers
(phase 1); Crissman and Solomon (phase 2)

Leatherworks, London
Client Sunar Ltd – UK sister company of Sunar
Hauserman   *Architect* Michael Graves   *Associate architect*
Jestico and Whiles   *Contractor* Morgan Lovell

Tiefenbrunnen Mill, Zurich, Switzerland
Client The Brothers Wehrli   *Architect* Pierre Zoelly
Collaborating architect Karl Holenstein   *Structural engineer*
Benno Bernardi   *Conservation architect* D. Nievergelt
Interior designer (for restaurant and miller's studio)
Gerd Burla

Lemsford Mill, Welwyn Garden City, UK
Client Michael Ayling of Lemsford Mill Controls Ltd
Architect Aldington Craig & Collinge   *Partner in charge*
Paul Collinge   *Project architect* Paul Collinge   *Structural
engineer* John Austin of Structures & Services Partnership
Main contractor H. J. & A. Wright   *Landscaping*
Clifton Nurseries

New Mills, Wotton-under-Edge, UK
Clients Renishaw Metrology – representative Andrew
Beasley   *Architect* Nial Phillips Associates   *Partner in charge*
Nial Phillips   *Project architect* Gillian Amos (phase 1); David
Caird (phase 2)   *Structural engineer* Roughton & Fenton
Main contractor Jotcham & Kendall (phase 1); Rush
& Tompkins (phase 2)

Lone Star Brewery, San Antonio, USA
Clients The San Antonio Museum of Art, San Antonio
Museum Association   *Architects* Cambridge Seven   *Principal
architect* Peter Chermayeff   *Project architect* Richard Tuve
Associate architect Chumney, Jones & Kell   *Museum designer*
Stuart Silver   *Structural engineer* LeMessurier Associates
SCI   *General contractor* Guido Brothers Construction
Company

Municipal Asphalt Plant, New York
Clients New York City Department of General Services; The
Neighborhood Committee for the Asphalt Green, Dr George
Murphy   *Architects* Hellmuth, Obata & Kassabaum,
Pasanella & Klein *Consultants (interiors)* Pasanella & Klein
Structural engineer Robert Silman Associates   *General
contractor* Series Contracting Corporation

Chewing Gum and Battery factories, New York
Owner Lazard Development Coporation   *Master plan* I. M.
Pei   *Architect* Gwathmey Siegel & Associates   *In association
with* Stephen Lepp Associates   *Design architect* Gwathmey
Siegel & Associates   *Associate in charge* Bruce Donnally
Structural engineer Berkenfeld-Getz Associates
Construction manager George A. Fuller Company

Templeton Factory, Glasgow, UK
Client The Scottish Development Agency   *Architect* The
Charles Robertson Partnership   *Structural engineer* A. M.
Sidey & Associates

Ligure Latta Factory, Genoa, Italy
Client Comune di Genova   *Architects* Fausto Colombo,
Guido Veneziani   *Structural engineers* Silvana di Stefano,
Guido Mazzone   *Contractor* Cattaneo S.p.A.

Ecclesiastical Buildings

Charles Street Meeting House, Boston, USA
Client Charles Street Meeting House Associates   *Architect*
John Sharratt Associates Inc.   *Principal in charge* John A.
Sharratt   *Structural engineers* Brown, Rona Inc.   *Contractors*
Sid Kumins Inc., Gentel Construction

Theosophical Temple, Amsterdam
Client Institution of Public Libraries, Amsterdam *Architects/ Interior designers* Bolhuis/Lambeck *Contractor* Public Works Service, Building Department

St Oswald's Old Church, Fulford, UK
Client Roy Grant *Architect* Anthony Richardson & Partners *Partner in charge* P. J. Lorimer *Specialist woodwork* A. T. Parry *Specialist glazing* Keith Barley *Site engineer* C. Richardson *Contractor* Kilvington & Young Limited

St James the Less, St Peter Port, Guernsey
Owner State of Guernsey *Designer/Architects* Bramall, Aylward, Sandwith Associates *Project architect* George Bramall *Contractor* C. A. Duquemin Ltd

Hospitalet Church, Ibiza
Client Ministry of Culture *Architects* José Antonio Martinez Lapeña, Elias Torres *Collaborating architects* Imma Josemaria, Moisés Martinez Lapeña, Benjamin Plequezueclos, Marcos Viader *Surveyor* Victor Mari

Kloster Petershausen, Constance, West Germany
Overall owner and client City of Constance *Owner and client for barrack-block, Land* of Baden-Württemberg *Winners of architectural competition for whole site and architects in overall charge* Ernst Friedrich Krieger & Lothar Greulich *Landscape consultants* Stadtbauplan Kindinger; Professor Gunnar Martinsson *Developer of loval government offices* Neue Heimat Städtebau *Architects for local government offices* Ernst Friedrich Krieger & Lothar Greulich *Owner and developer for new housing* WOBAK (Construction company of the City of Constance) *Owner and developer for new housing* LAWOG (Construction company for housing in the *Land* Baden-Württemberg) *Architects for new housing* Stockburger – Späth – Dickmann *Contractor for housing* Paul Brenner; Konstanzer Spar- und Bauverein

Charterhouse of Ittingen, Thurgau, Switzerland
Client Foundation Charterhouse, Ittingen *Architect renovating the church* Scherrer & Hartung, SIA/FSAI *Architect for the museum* Antoniol & Huber Dpl. Architekten ETH/SIA *Architects* R. & E. Guyer *Project architect* Fredi Zwahlen

Rural Buildings

Old Surgery, Wantage, UK
Owner Vale of the White Horse District Council *Management* Vale and Downland Museum Trust *Architect* Brian Hubble and Partners

Leatheringsett Hill, Holt, UK
Client Mr P. H. Roberts *Architects/designer* Michael R. Pert *Builder* D. Morrissey

Hospitalet de Llobregat, Barcelona, Spain
Client Catalonian Library Service *Architects* Martorell, Bohigas and Mackay

Stone barn, St Andrew, Guernsey
Owner BASA Ltd *Architect* Bramall, Aylward, Sandwith Associates *Project architect* Richard Sandwith *Structural engineers* Andrews, Kent & Stone *Contractor* F. Watson & Son Ltd

Malthouse granary, Hadleigh, UK
Client Babergh District Council *Architect* Arup Associates *Engineer* Arup Associates *Main contractor* Sindall Construction Ltd

Chatelherault, Hamilton, UK
Owners Hamilton District Council, Historic Buildings & Monuments Directorate, Scottish Development Department *Architect* Geoffrey Jarvis, formerly of the Boys Jarvis Partnership *Project architects* Roger Fleming (until 1982); Paul O'Neill (from 1982) *Structural and civil engineers* D. M. Doig & Smith *Main contractor* Stewart McGlashen Limited *Stone supplier* Stewart McGlashen Limited *Plastering contractor* Leonard Stead & Co.

The Menagerie, Horton, UK
Owner Gervase Jackson Stops *Plan drawing for original work and extensions* Jean Jackson Stops *Freehand plasterwork* Christopher Hobbs *Other plasterwork* Leonard Stead & Son *Designer of portico* Charles Morris

Further Reading

Alte Bauten neu genutzt, P. Anstett, H. Fecher et al., Deutsche Verlags-Anstalt, Stuttgart, 1981.
Architectural Conservation in Europe, S. Cantacuzino (ed.), Architectural Press, London, 1975.
Aspects of Conservation One, New Life for Old Buildings, Department of the Environment, Scottish Development Department, Welsh Office, HMSO, London, 1971.
Aspects of Conservation Three, New Life for Old Churches, Department of the Environment, Scottish Development Department, Welsh Office, HMSO, London, 1977.
Bâtiments Anciens – Usages Nouveaux : 1, Images du Possible, Paris, 1979; *2, Quelques Exemples par l'Animation Culturelle*, Centre National d'Art et de Culture Georges Pompidou, L'Association Etudes et Cultures, Paris (undated).
Britain's Historic Buildings : a Policy for their Future Use, Lord Montagu of Beaulieu, British Tourist Authority, London, 1980.
Building Conservation and Rehabilitation : Designing for Change in Building Use, T. A. Markus (ed.), Butterworths, London, 1979.
Building Legislation and Historic Buildings, English Heritage, Architectural Press, London, 1987.
Built to last : a Handbook on Recycling Old Buildings, G. Bunnel, Preservation Press/National Trust for Historic Preservation, Washington, D.C., 1977.
The Care of Old Buildings Today, D. Insall, Architectural Press, London, 1972.
I Centri Storici : Rimini, Firenze, P. L. Cervellati and M. Miliari, Guaraldi, Rimini, 1977.
Change of Use : the Conversion of Old Buildings, P. Cunnington, Alpha Books (A. & C. Black), London, 1988.
Conversion : a Credit Account, M. Pearce, SAVE Britain's Heritage, London, 1988.

Conservation as Cultural Survival : Proceedings of the Seminar held in Istanbul, Turkey, 26-28 September 1978, Aga Khan Award for Architecture, Geneva, 1979.

Conservation of Historic Buildings, B. M. Feilden, Butterworths Scientific, London, 1982.

The Country House : to be or not to be, M. Binney and K. Martin, SAVE Britain's Heritage, McGraw-Hill, London, 1982.

Créer dans le Créé : l'Architecture Contemporaine dans les Bâtiments Anciens, ICOMOS/France, Electa Moniteur, Paris, 1986.

A Critical Bibliography of Building Conservation, J. F. Smith, Mansell, London, 1978.

Dal Piccolo al Grande Restauro, P. Marconi, Marsilio Editori, Venice, 1988.

Financing the Preservation of Old Buildings, Civic Trust, London, 1971.

Financing the Use of Old Buildings : a Practical Guide to Sources of Finance, Materials and Labour for Projects involving the Provision of Workspace, URBED, London, 1979.

A Future for Farm Buildings, G. Darley, SAVE Britain's Heritage, London, 1988.

A Future from the Past the Case for Conservation and Re-use of Old Buildings in Industrial Communities, R. Langenbach, US Department of Housing and Urban Development/ Massachusetts Department of Community Affairs, Washington, D.C., 1977.

Guidelines for Conservation : a Technical Manual, B. M. Feilden, INTACH, New Delhi, 1989.

Historic Preservation : Curatorial Management of the Built World, J. M. Fitch, McGraw-Hill, New York, 1982.

An Introduction to Conservation, B. M. Feilden, UNESCO, New York, 1979.

Neues Leben für alte Bauten : Über den Continuo in der Architektur, G. Müller-Menckens, Verlagsanstalt Alexander Koch, Stuttgart, 1977.

The New Museum : Architecture and Display, M. Brawne, Architectural Press, London, 1965.

New Profits from Old Buildings, R. M. Warner, S. M. Groff and R. P. Warner, McGraw-Hill, New York, 1979.

New Uses for Old Buildings, S. Cantacuzino, Architectural Press, London, 1975.

New Uses for Older Buildings in Scotland, Scottish Civic Trust, HMSO, Edinburgh, 1981.

Our Architectural Heritage from Consciousness to Conservation, C. Erder, UNESCO, New York, 1986.

Re-using Railroad Stations (2 vols.), Educational Facilities Laboratories, Washington, D.C., 1974/75.

Re-using Redundant Buildings : Case Studies of Good Practice in Urban Regeneration, URBED (Urban and Economic Development) Ltd, HMSO, London, 1987.

Reviving Old Buildings and Communities, M. Talbot, David & Charles, Newton Abbot, 1986.

Saving Old Buildings, S. Cantacuzino and Susan Brandt, Architectural Press, London, 1980.

Urbino : la Storia di una Città e il Piano della sua Evoluzione Urbanistica, G. De Carlo, Marsilio, Padua, 1966.

L'Utilisation des monuments historiques, D. Mandelkern, Caisse Nationale des Monuments Historiques et des Sites, Paris, 1979.

Working Places : the Adaptive Use of Older Buildings, W. Kidney, Ober Park Associates, Pittsburgh, 1976.

Acknowledgments

First and foremost, I want to acknowledge the invaluable support given me by my wife, Anne, who accompanied me on my journeys, typed the manuscripts, and generally acted as editorial assistant. Without her the book would never have seen the light of day.

I must refer with very special gratitude for their help in America to Lisa and Bertrand Taylor, Peter Palumbo, Kathy and Boone Powell of San Antonio, Professor David Woodcock of A & M University, Mesfin Samuel of Dallas, Martha Lampkin of Sasaki Associates, and James Goode, the distinguished art historian, who generously put his time and encyclopaedic knowledge of Washington at my disposal; for their help in France to Karen Longeteig and Hasan Uddin Khan, Dr Brian Brace-Taylor, Ionel Schein and Maurice Culot, Director of the Institut Français d'Architecture in Paris; for their help in Italy to Conte Luigi and Contessa Nicky Cadorna, Giovanni and Jennifer Grego and Professor Hilda Selem of the University of Rome; for their help in Austria to Susan and Desmond Bowen, Professor Hans Hollein and Dr Gerhard Sailer, President of the Bundesdenkmalamt in Vienna; for their help in Switzerland to Fredi and Béatrice Mülethaler-Roy, Farrokh Derekshani, Pierre Zoelly, Gilbert Frey and H. Rusterholz of Metron, architects for the conversion of the paper mill at Küttingen; for their help in Germany to Graf Michael and Gräfin Ileana Metternich, and Bürgermeister Ralf-Joachim Fischer of Constance.

I also want to mention gratefully Mildred Schmertz, editor of the *Architectural Record*; Joseph Lombardi, architect in New York; Dennis Frenchman of Lane, Frenchman & Associates, designer of the Lowell National Historic Park and co-author of the original master plan; Dr Thomas Costello, Vice-President of the University of Lowell and the University's co-ordinator of the University of Lowell Master Plan; Sarah Peskin, Planning Director of the Lowell Historic Preservation Commission; Walker C. Johnson, architect in Chicago; Wilbert R. Hasbrouck of Hasbrouck Peterson Associates, architects for the conversion of Dearborn Station in Chicago; Gary Skotnicki of Archi Texas, architects for the conversion of the Turtle Creek Pump Station in Dallas; the Ogelsby Group, architects for the conversion of the Sanger-Harris department store in Dallas; W. O. Neuhaus, architect for the conversion of the Star Engraving Building in Houston; David Jones of Martin and Jones, architects for the conversion of the East Capitol Car Barn in Washington; Hamilton and Terry Morton, architect and art historian in Washington; Arthur Cotton Moore, architect in Washington; David H. Gleason, architect in Baltimore; Nicholas Brown, Director of the Baltimore Aquarium; Nicholas Falk, Director of URBED; Amanda Levete and Pierre Botschi of the Richard Rogers Partnership, architects for the conversion of Billingsgate Market in London; Ernest Hall, creator and director of the Dean Clough Industrial Park in Halifax; Kirsty and Dick Squires; J. H. Rae, Director of Planning, City of Glasgow; E. Moriarty of the architects' department, Cork County Council; Claus Brunotte of Siemens Ag., Munich; Michael Alder, architect for the conversion of the paper-drying warehouse in St Albantal, Basle; Guido Canali, architect in Parma; Andrea Bruno, architect in Turin; and Roberto Einaudi, architect for the restoration and conversion of the Palazzo Massimo alle Colonne in Rome.

My gratitude goes also to Bruce M. Kriviskey, Director, Historic Preservation Programs of the American Institute of Architects; Sally Oldham, Vice-President, Preservation Programs, National Trust for Historic Preservation; Susan Anable, Collections Manager, National Trust for Historic Preservation; Marilyn Jordan Taylor, partner in Skidmore, Owings & Merrill, New York; Michael Trostel, architect in Baltimore; Robert G. Neily, architect in Boston; Anthony C. Coombes of Olympia & York in London; Marianne Malonne and Charmian Marshall of the Europa Nostra secretariat in London; Caroline Miérop, Director of the Foundation for Architecture in Brussels; Emil van Brederöde, Secretary, ICOMOS (Netherlands); Björn Linn, Professor of Architecture at Chalmers University, Göteborg; Museum of Finnish Architecture, Helsinki; Dr Samir Abdulac, Director, Conseil d'Architecture d'Urbanisme et de l'Environnement (CAUE), Eure et Loire; Stefano Bianca, architect in Zurich; Ugo Brunoni, architect in Geneva; Professor Bruno Zevi, architect and Member of Parliament in Rome; David Mackay of Martorell, Bohigas & Mackay, architects in Barcelona; and Fernando Ramón, architect in Madrid.

It would be impossible to list all the people who have helped on a book of this kind, but any acknowledgment would be inadequate if I failed to thank all the owners, developers and architects whose buildings are included and who greatly facilitated my task by providing me with the necessary information and material. I must also thank Ruth Kamen and her staff at the RIBA library for their unfailing courtesy and assistance in tracing published material. To my publishers, Thames and Hudson, I am much indebted, and to Anne Engel I am grateful for having proposed the book and the author in the first place.

Index

Italic numerals refer to pages on which illustrations occur, and **bold** numerals to special features on individual schemes.